Electronic Chronicles

Electronic Chronicles
Columns of the Changes in Our Time

Paul Levinson, Ph.D.

Anamnesis Press
Tallahassee, Florida

Library of Congress Cataloging-in-Publication Data

Levinson, Paul.
 Electronic chronicles: columns of the changes in our time / by
Paul Levinson.

    p.cm.
   Includes index.
   ISBN 0-9631203-3-6: $14.95
   1. Computers and civilization. 2. Telecommunication—Social
aspects. I. Title.
QA76.9.C66L48 1992
303.48'33—dc20   92-18689
                                                            CIP

Anamnesis Press
P.O. Box 14304
Tallahassee, FL 32317

for Molly and Simon, and for Tina
— and for Isaac Asimov

TABLE OF CONTENTS

PRESS ENTER:
A WORD FROM THE PUBLISHER

This unusual book by Dr. Paul Levinson of the New School for Social Research is truly a product of the Computer Age. Not only does it collect a series of "electronic columns" originally composed on the computer and transmitted to readers throughout the world via modem and global telecommunications networks — making it one of the first books of its kind — but the physical volume itself was typeset, designed, edited and produced with the aid of a state-of-the-art desktop microcomputer.

What's more, the computer played still another role in the chain of circumstances that made this book a reality. Via GEnie, the General Electric network for information exchange, Dr. Levinson first became acquainted with Anamnesis Press and brought the Chronicles to our attention. Through the medium of the computer telecommunications network we maintained a continual dialog on every aspect of the book's production.

Computers: as a scientist, I find them immensely useful for experimental design and data analysis. As a poet, I find them surprisingly utilitarian, and not at all the anathema to inspiration that many had feared. (A number of speculative and imaginative poets — myself included — have actually composed collaborative poems via the major commercial computer networks such as GEnie, and the results have been quite satisfying.)

As a publisher, I find computers indispensable; Anamnesis Press would not exist without them. Computers have even made it possible for the non-artist to produce graphic designs that compete with the best designs of artists and professional graphic designers. The cover of this book is a good example of the power of graphic design software.

To claim that computers — and the electronic media they engender — have changed our world irrevocably would belabor the obvious. Better than most, Paul Levinson understands the effects of computers and telecommunications media on each and every one of us. He possesses the same visionary sense of wonder

that characterizes the finest science fiction writers of our time —
writers like Isaac Asimov and Arthur C. Clarke — a vision that
makes them such perfect commentators on 20th century change
and progress.

Levinson, a science fiction writer at heart, is clearly excited
by the possibilities inherent in the thoughtful application of
technology, and demonstrates keen insights into the effects that
rapid technological change have had on world events. A philosopher at home in a wide range of media, from the modem to the
printed page, he analyzes, conjectures, dreams, explains — and
entertains. Press enter, and enjoy.

Keith Allen Daniels
New Haven, CT
February, 1992

PREFACE

The following is a series of electronic columns — essays and commentaries — begun for the Western Behavioral Sciences Institute's online School of Management and Strategic Studies in September of 1985. WBSI was headquartered in La Jolla, California, but its computer network attracted people from all over the world. In July 1987, I stopped writing these for WBSI, but have continued the series for Connected Education and The New School OnLine Program — a computer network that has participants from some 15 nations around the world.

The themes of these columns range from discussion of personal computers and their impact on our lives, to assessment of major technological events such as the Challenger and Chernobyl disasters, to consideration of the popular culture and philosophy of television and rock 'n' roll. Many of the columns were written within hours or days after political, pop cultural, or technological events, and they thus constitute a log of response to some of the most significant developments in the 1985-1991 period. The initial mode of publication of these chronicles — in which people from around the world received them via personal computers and modems, directly in their homes and places of business, often minutes after the essays were written — provides in itself a vivid example of the new type of "virtual" or "cyber" community that has arisen in the past decade, and is becoming an increasingly important player in our personal and professional lives.

In my first chronicle — "Chronicle Ecology" (written in September, 1985) — I say that I will be writing and posting a new chronicle once a week. However, reality, even when electronically engendered, seldom equals all expectations, and thus the real frequency of the Chronicles in the past seven years has often been much less (especially so in the past few years). The Chronicles are presented in this volume in the same order in which they first appeared online, and I have refrained from rewriting with the exception of a minor stylistic adjustment here and there. The only systematic differences between these and the online Chronicles are parenthetical pointers in this text to later chronicles on a similar theme, and footnotes marked "January, 1992" at the conclusion of given chronicles to indicate events that have occurred and information that I have obtained relevant to these chronicles since their original publication.

Because the Chronicles are in chronological order, the themes are fairly well homogenized throughout this volume. However, since the summer of 1989 ("Preamble to Soviet Chronicles") the focus of all 10 essays save one ("Telewar" — on the role of television in the Gulf War) has been on the informational and media aspects of what we now know was the final political disintegration of the Soviet Union. The last chronicle in this volume — "'JFK' and Gorbachev" — is the only one written with knowledge of this volume, and was written just yesterday, the day after New Year's.

Paul Levinson
New York City
January, 1992

P.S.: I have also added several "May, 1992" footnotes to chronicles relevant to events that have occurred in the early months of 1992.

TRADEMARKS AND OTHER NAMES
APPEARING IN THE CHRONICLES

Many of the Chronicles make reference to organizations that are or were part of the online community in which the Chronicles were written. Most of these references are clear in the context of the text, but the major ones are listed below, along with their trademark status where applicable and other information.

CompuServe: trademarked name of commercial online network (Compuserve Inc., an H & R Block Company).

Connect Ed, Connected Education: trademarked names of the services provided by Connected Education, Inc., a not-for-profit corporation (President, Paul Levinson; Vice President, Tina Vozick) that offers online courses for academic credit in conjunction with the New School for Social Research, and engages in other online activities including consulting and electronic publishing. Chronicles have appeared on the Connect Ed online campus since September 1986, and exclusively since July 1987.

COSY: trademarked name for Computer Conferencing System (Cosy Systems Group, University of Guelph, Canada)

EIES: trademarked name of the Electronic Information Exchange System of the New Jersey Institute of Technology (Newark, NJ). This was the online computer conferencing system upon which the Connect Ed electronic campus was situated from 1985-1991, and upon which WBSI (see below) activities took place from 1982-1989. EIES ceased operation in October 1991 (succeeded by EIES2). Connect Ed left EIES in August 1991, and created a new electronic campus on the PARTI system on Unison (see below).

GEnie: trademarked name of the General Electric Network for Information Exchange (commercial network) (General Electric Co.)

PARTI, Participate: trademarked names of a commercial computer conferencing system (Participate Technologies LP), situated on The Source (and other online systems) until July 1989, and thereafter on CompuServe and other online systems. Since August 1991, Connected Education has been operating on the PARTI system on Unison (see below).

Prodigy: trademarked name of commercial online network (Prodigy Services Co., a partnership of IBM and Sears).

The Source: trademarked name of commercial online system, acquired by CompuServe in 1989.

Unison: commercial online network (Applied Software Designs, Inc.) upon which the Connect Ed online campus and the Electronic Chronicles have been situated since August 1991.

WBSI: Western Behavioral Sciences Institute commissioned the start of the Chronicles in 1985 (where they continued online through July 1987); WBSI ceased operations in the Fall of 1991.

CHRONICLE ECOLOGY

Harold Innis, Canada's favorite economist and mentor of Marshall McLuhan, was one of the first to observe that the health of societies requires a balance of time-binding and space-extending media. Our individual capacities to store and transmit information are best complemented by devices that assist both memory and dispersion, and Innis saw the rise and fall of civilizations as largely a story of balance and unbalance in communication — of a too strong penchant for either preservation or dissemination eventually undoing a once robust community. Thus, Egypt crumbled under the weight of its obsession with the past, and Rome spent itself in flings to the far corners of its world. But the Renaissance flowered in the mixture of recording and exchange made possible by the printing press.

Print on paper is a good medium for achievement of a time/space balance, for it both endures and is easy to move. Beyond the technology itself is the human decision about how to apply it, and in the 19th century the leisurely journal was a great counterpoint to the fast newspaper and the slow book. Journals, weeklies, monthlies, chronicles of all sorts actually first proliferated in the 1840s as a product of the new highly productive printing presses, often left with time on their handles as book runs proceeded much faster than expected. The periodical proved the perfect item to produce with this extra time. And soon the journal came to typify the contemplative Victorian culture that engendered so much of our 20th century science and technology.

Can the commentative, Victorian flavor of a journal be recreated and re-presented in the lightning atmosphere of electronic creation and communication of text? Well, one thing we know is that new wine in old media bottles always tastes a lot different than the old wine. One of the goals of this column — Electronic Chronicles — is to see just how different the leisurely journal will be, electronically presented.

This is not the very first time such a journal has been done. Walt Roberts' excellent "Provocations" is an example of how the scientific weekly commentary can flourish in an electronic format.*

Think of this as a technological, philosophic, social cousin to Walt's "Provocations." Here we will chronicle the cutting edge of communications technologies, with special attention to how they change the way we know, feel, and live in this world. As befits a journal, I will enter one essay a week for your perusal. As also befits a journal, your letters to the editor will be welcome here (and of course will be published here instantly upon your entry of them as comments in this conference). And as befits a Victorian editor, I may from time to time respond to one or two of your letters.

The fragmentation and specialization that is sooner or later the lot of general interest media, as well as the appeal of easy radio and TV, long ago put *The Popular Science Monthly* and *Harper's* out of business. Strange as it may be for us rarefied breed of computer conferencers to contemplate, this medium of computer conferencing that we're now in is a prime example of an early, generalized form of a medium — one that has the capacity to appeal to tastes undeadened by doctrinaire adherence to narrow academic disciplines.

I invite you to invite me into your library or study once each week, fireplace crackling or cool breeze blowing through the window, as we think about the recreation of our world through technology.

---

*January, 1992 — Walter Orr Roberts — eminent climatologist, co-author of the "nuclear winter" scenario book (*The Cold and the Dark*, 1984), and a leading researcher and discussant of the "greenhouse effect" — continued his online "Provocations" on a weekly basis until his death in January, 1990. He is an example of the best of what online communication can do in many ways — not least of all for me being that he became my colleague and friend even though we never met in person and spoke on the phone but a handful of times. He was the first distinguished scholar to offer some of his writings to the Connected Education OnLine Library — in this case, his "Provocations" — and our Library was renamed in his honor in January, 1990.

GLOBALISM AND INDEPENDENT INVENTION

Among the most intriguing events in the history of technology is the incidence of multiple independent, often nearly simultaneous, invention of the same devices. Friese-Greene in England, Edison in the U.S., and the Lumières in France all developed motion picture devices pretty much around the same time and in more or less ignorance of one another. Alexander Graham Bell beat Elisha Gray to the U.S. Patent Office with the telephone by a mere matter of hours(!) — (just think, if things had gone differently, we'd now be talking about Baby Grays). They knew only vaguely of each other's work. And historians are still wrangling about whether it was really Fust, not Gutenberg, who first introduced the idea of movable type in Europe.

These examples of independent invention are powerful arguments in favor of an evolutionary theory of culture and technology which says that when the culture or society or intellectual or business climate is ready for a certain device, it will "select" it into existence by encouraging anyone who is in a position to do so to invent it. A great irony is that the communication devices that resulted from this evolutionary process are obliterating the very social environment that made this process possible. As global communication becomes increasingly efficient, fewer and fewer places are left in which to be ignorant of others' work and in that sense independent.

What effect will this have on the pace and quality of invention? Can the much lamented decrease in American inventiveness be laid to some extent at the open door of too much information about what other companies and countries are up to? Would we be better off if we deliberately ignored what our competitors are doing, and paid more attention to the rhythms of our own drums?

Well, students of human cognition have long noticed that a certain "nursery" period, when the thinker is cut off or protected from outside criticism and indeed outside reports of similar work, may be helpful and even necessary in the generation of new ideas.

I once knew a professor who would get furious if anyone even spoke to her about work similar to what she was writing about once her book got beyond a certain point. (Actually, as far as I know, she never did finish the one book she was working on.)

It well may be that a genius too soon exposed to another's similar work might get discouraged, and leave unfinished a product that completed in isolation would have been superior to its rival. Or, premature contact with a body of work more advanced than one's own might lead to acceptance of conclusions from the advanced work that in fact might prove to be incorrect, and therefore destructive of the less developed work.

Nonetheless, there may be another side to this story. Edison's desire to exceed the success of Bell proved to be one of the great motivating factors in Edison's life, with spectacular consequences for the age of invention. The capacity to integrate another's invention into your own agenda, and use it as a platform upon which to attain new heights, takes a genius of its own, perhaps not as original as the ability to invent something from isolated scratch, but ultimately perhaps just as far-reaching in its results.

In any case, we as a culture do not have much choice in the matter. The era of the idiosyncratic inventor in the garage is largely gone — even Wozniak and Jobs are long gone from Apple — and in its place is the integrated leapfrogger who thrives in a maximum flow of information. Once opened by technologies of instant and enduring communication, the gates to information will never again be closed.

Friese-Greene wound up haunted and unsatisfied by his discovery that Edison had invented the flick at the same time as he. His remaining years were spent in a generally futile attempt to develop a color motion picture process. Who knows how much sooner color photography would have been perfected had Friese-Greene known of Edison's work on motion pictures earlier, and devoted his time from the beginning to achievement of a color process?

INTERRUPTIONS:
IN NATURE AND TECHNOLOGY

My educational activities suffered two dramatic interruptions this week. The first was when EIES (the Electronic Information Exchange System — the computer network upon which Connected Education is situated) went down for more than twenty-four hours this past Tuesday-Wednesday. The second occurred when Fairleigh Dickinson University and The New School for Social Research joined the rest of the NYC metropolitan area in a shutdown on Friday in preparation for Hurricane Gloria, who fortunately turned out to be pretty much of a weak sister in many places up here.

It is interesting to compare our reactions to each of these extraordinary events.

The day-long crash of EIES was greeted by annoyance and even anger by some. A general feeling that EIES or someone at EIES was in some sense responsible for this breakdown, and ought to be blamed, seemed apparent in several people with whom I communicated since. The EIES staff itself seemed to share this feeling on some level, going to the unusual trouble of putting up an online sign-on apology.

The shutdown of New York City in preparation for Hurricane Gloria was on the other hand greeted as a prudent, even courageous and brilliant, move. Mayor Koch appeared on TV as the dauntless David standing up to this squalling Goliath that threatened us all. Although the hurricane in fact failed to materialize with anything like the force predicted, all parties (quite correctly) clapped themselves on the back for acting so expeditiously.

Why do we expect so much of our technology and so little of nature? Why is a shutdown of a computer system to avert a worse disruption accorded such little patience, while the shutdown of a whole coast to avoid a potential natural disaster applauded as wise and timely?

Well, we are ultimately responsible for our technologies in a way that we cannot be (as yet) for nature: we after all create the technologies, whereas nature created us. Yet the parenthood of a process has little if any effect on its tendency to occasionally break down or go wrong — a tendency intrinsic in all events in this universe, natural or technological. So welcome to the ubiquity of noise, to use a term from engineering. No matter how carefully we design a technological system, no matter how fully we think we understand a natural phenomenon, we will always sooner or later discover something of great importance that we overlooked. History persists in showing that even the best system, even the most fully corroborated theory, will sooner or later come up short. Logic tells us that even though we may develop processes to reduce noise, these processes can never eliminate noise or error completely, for they carry an error quotient of their own. Likelihood of breakdowns can be reduced, but never to zero. This propensity for error is far more pervasive than the human fallibilism that many religions stress: it seems woven into the very fabric of all existence.

And indeed, one of the prime purposes of technology is to provide back up systems when noise crops up in a system we're using. These back-up technologies of course have bugs of their own, but if they're capable of performing when other systems fail, they make a real contribution to the continuity and satisfaction of human life.

Speaking of which, I was able to put in a full day's work and more on Friday. Though schools and roads were closed, and the city wrapped up tighter than a drum, I had no trouble logging on to this computer system.

REQUIEM FOR A MEDIUM?

I was talking on the phone before, and that started me thinking again about why we've yet to commercialize and distribute in any widespread way the videophone. Few media have been predicted as imminent successors as often as the picture telephone, and few media have disappointed so consistently.

In my "Human Replay: A Theory of the Evolution of Media" (1979), I termed the videophone the aging heir apparent. Novelized as early as 1914 in Victor Appleton's *Tom Swift and His Photo-Telephone*; utilized by a Presidential candidate in 1928 in the first big test of television (which was conceived in those days as a telephone with pictures); darling of the 1939 World's Fair (in which the computer received not a sliver of a mention); done up slick in late '50s and early '60s advertising as Bell's "Picturephone" — and yet all to little or no avail.

What went wrong?

Some say it's a question of modesty. A student recently told me that a great advantage of online education was that she could attend my class in her bathrobe, and videoconferencing certainly would deprive her of that luxury. And yet a species as inventive as ours surely could figure out the equivalent of window shades for the window phone. We could, for example, simply put up a smiling freeze frame of us which would serve as our display for our callers whenever we wished to remain off-camera. We could call this a "modesty" panel and call it forth by the push of a button.

Others emphasize the political problems — folks do not feel good about homes filled with video cameras which in principle could transmit their pictures to the eager eyes of government Peeping Toms. But has not the clout of this argument dissipated somewhat with the quiet passing of 1984, sans Big Brother?

I used to argue that the videophone was scotched by oppressive Federal regulations which kept the telephone company by and large out of the television and thereby the video business. I don't care much for Federal regulation anyway, and this seemed as good an explanation as any.

But divestiture — the splitting of AT&T's monopoly and the trade-off it received in terms of permission to pursue virtually any business it chose — has exonerated Federal restraint as the villain of at least this story.

And so we have the surprising case of words — text — as the first real product to be exchanged via interactive screens. Perhaps not so surprising after all, when we recall that electrons were used in the service of printed words via telegraph long before they were harnessed for spoken words in telephones and radio, and images via television.

And yet the videophone and its extension the videoconference remain on the edge of many expectations about the future of this online text medium we're now using. Wait until we get better image resolution, wait until we can easily send pictures of people's faces into everyone's terminals, wait until the cheapest CRT can show diagrams with full photographic accuracy, some observers say — THAT will be when the online network really achieves its stride as a communicative tool.

I'm actually a great fan of videophone, in *Star Trek* and boardrooms alike, and I think it will one day achieve at least part of its long held promise.

But as a successor to electronic text interaction? Even Herbert Hoover would have known better.

AI ON THE SHINGLE

A friend recently gave me a demonstration of an interesting AI (artificial intelligence) medical diagnosis program. Worked right on a personal computer, something like this:

The program asks you to pick as many symptoms as you feel are appropriate from a list of several hundred that scroll on the screen. Symptoms include headache, nausea, etc.

At the end of this round, you have the option of asking the program to display all diseases that might give rise to these chosen symptoms. For example, if you indicated headache, the disease list at this point would likely include everything from tension to brain tumor.

The program next asks you a series of questions about each of the symptoms you picked. How long, in terms of days, weeks, or months, or years, have you had these headaches? How long, in terms of minutes, hours, etc., do each of these bouts usually last? Are the headaches accompanied by nausea, by blurriness of vision, etc.

Again, at any point in the questioning, you can request a diagnosis based on the answers you've supplied. The diagnosis comes in a list of possible diseases, which grows shorter with every additional answer you supply.

After about 40 minutes of this procedure, the program narrowed the diagnosis down to two or three very similar diseases. (In one case, though, the final candidates were very dissimilar — one guy was told he had either an ulcer or stomach cancer.)

As far as I know, programs like this are used only as assistants to human doctors, not replacements.

But the issue is clearly drawn: there may soon come a time when CAD (computer assisted diagnosis) turns out to be more accurate than human-only diagnosis. What will happen then? Will human doctors be subject to malpractice suits because they didn't call in the services of an AI medical program?

Will AI engineers be liable for the faulty diagnoses of their programs? Would that be fair? Do we hold medical schools legally responsible for faulty diagnoses by the human doctors they train?

Whose judgement will prevail when machine and human doctor disagree? Will a machine or a human be called in for a second opinion, and if both, who will prevail should silicon and carbon disagree again?

The advantages and disadvantages of machine augmentation and/or substitution of human performance are pretty much the same regardless of the tasks under consideration: Machines do not get drunk, are not distracted by affairs of the heart, do not get bored by repetition, do not start work in a bad mood because of an argument with the spouse in the morning. But machines presumably lack the capacity for the left-field (right brained) cognitive leaps of judgement that come so easily to humans — we humans can instantly recognize blue blotches on the hand as the result of a leaky pen rather than an exotic skin disease, for example.

In the life and death realm of medical diagnosis, these issues take on the sharpest possible definition, and boil down to this: Are more lives jeopardized through the use of machine experts in diagnoses, or more lives jeopardized by not availing ourselves of the benefits of this expert analysis?

The fate of the AI patient may hold a prognosis for AI that goes far beyond medicine.

PHILOSOPHY IN SF CLOTHING

We're accustomed in our enlightened age to find knowledge only in the halls of academe and the products of formal training. Engineers and hands-on programmers seem to have the most right to take part in the profound dialogues concerning artificial intelligence and robotics (can machines think, what is thought, etc.), and academically official philosophers are occasionally begrudged an audience. Douglas Hofstadter (author of *Gödel, Escher, Bach*), who satisfies neither criterion, but who has made a crucial contribution in pointing out the differences between constructing intelligences from the top down (the current expert systems approach) and the bottom up (build stupid inexact systems and let them evolve into higher intelligence), has a hard time finding acceptance in the scholarly establishment.

Isaac Asimov has it even worse. Yet his short stories on robots written as early as the 1940s make him a full contemporary of such acknowledged pioneers in AI as Turing, von Neumann, and Wiener. While von Neumann was constructing Turing's theoretical "universal machine" in a real computer, and Wiener was puzzling out the metaphysical implications of informational similarities in machines and organisms, Asimov was tackling the fascinating issues of free will and definition of human mentality in his Three Laws of Robotics. (First Law: A robot by action or inaction must never let any harm befall a human. Second Law: A robot must obey all human commands except when they contravene the first law. Third Law: A robot must seek to maintain its own wellbeing except when such pursuit contravenes the first two laws.) The inevitable failure of these laws to operate as intended provides the narrative excitement in Asimov's works, as well as some great disquisitions on the in-principle impossibilities of programming and design. In short, his stories must give pause to any who think that machines may be programmed the way we want them to behave with high degrees of intelligence — programming and real intelligence are ultimately incompatible in Asimov's world, as indeed they are in our world as well.

Should we be surprised to find such stuff in science fiction? Well, Jules Verne's predictions in the 19th century were more on target than any technological futurist of that period I know of (admittedly there were few). Wells' social predictions and analyses weren't too shoddy either, and writers like Stapledon provided some pretty good existential philosophy in the guise of science fiction in the 1930s. Maybe the problem in the last 40 years is that we're too quick to associate all science fiction with the slick, superficial genre that usually appears in the movies.

The writers themselves add to the problem. People who have great ideas often seem innocent of the importance of their own work. I remember receiving a charming note from Asimov years ago when I first sent him an essay I had published about his work. I love your analysis, he told me, but I had nothing quite so profound in mind when I first wrote this work.

Literary critics tell us that the author is the last person you should seek as a guide to the meaning of a work, yet fiction authors and artists are the antennae of our species nonetheless.

Applying this principle to science fiction would tap a pool of wisdom in our search for knowledge of ourselves and our world we can ill afford to ignore.

ONLINE EDUCATION
AND THE CASTLE WALLS

Online communities are prone to internal squabbling. The distance between angered brain and a fingertip on the keyboard is very short — especially late at night — and apparently not as subject to restraints that most of us have on our tongues. And thus a difference felt is often a difference expressed, online, and these can develop into "flamewars" at the drop of a warm boot.

Still, when I attend an in-person departmental meeting (aptly described by Stephen Jay Gould as among the most enervating experiences known to our species), or a conference with "colleagues" in my field, I'm reminded anew how minor are most of our online differences when compared to the differences between us — the online cognoscenti — and the rest of the world. In the world of education, at least, the fact is that most administrators and faculty know little of the online option. What they do know they're likely to misconstrue (a common error is viewing an online seminar, in which groups engage in dialogue for months at a time, as a "correspondence" class, in which one teacher deals with one student); and what they don't know they seem singularly uneager to learn.

Once upon a time, printers and readers of books were very much in the same boat. Misunderstood and even disliked in many cases by the leaders of Church, state, and the powers that were, the new book culture quietly gave rise to universities and intellectual communities that changed the shape of the world.

And now these towers of book culture loom over us, in many cases rigid and swollen with 400 years of hegemony. Education via computer conferencing couldn't commence at Harvard or Oxford or Princeton. They have too much invested in the past. And so the pioneers in the revolution came from unknown places like the Western Behavioral Sciences Institute, small schools like the New York Institute of Technology, mavericks like the New School for Social Research.

Nor was it an accident either that the computer system on which we launched our online program was based not at MIT or CalTech, but at the New Jersey Institute of Technology. It could have been no other way — MIT is too important to take such risks for the future.

Online education faces enormous obstacles. And I think the worst has yet to come. Success of the pioneer rarely satisfies the entrenched at first — such success, to the contrary, invites replacement of the backhanded slap with the frontal assault. As recently as 1984, a President of Harvard declared himself an opponent of computers in education (I wonder: had he ever been online?). What will come next? The notion that a student any place in the world can work with a scholar any place in the world — without either leaving their home or place of business or study — is unnerving with good cause to an educational system based on the university as the center of the universe.

Of course, that online notion of "distributed" education is barely realized at present. A revolution is, after all, an hypothesis — it may disintegrate due to internal inconsistency, may be mistaken in its view of reality, may die of many causes having nothing to do with the opposition of the establishment.

We shall see.

ON SCREAMING AT READERS

Several years ago, when I was editing *In Pursuit of Truth* (Humanities Press, 1982), I had occasion to write to a contributor of an egregiously esoteric piece on philosophy. So abstract and (to me) abstruse was this piece, that I suggested the use of italics in several places to make the meaning at least minimally comprehensible.

"Oh no, never italics," the contributor replied archly, "I don't believe in screaming at the reader."

Although my first instinct was to scream at *him*, I had to admit that he had something of a point. Eventually we agreed on non-italicized changes in the wording to make the meaning clear.

The tendency to want to do something to words to give them more force, more vividness, is especially acute in online writing. The closest analogues to online discussion are phone and in-person conversations on the one hand, and old-fashioned letters on the other. All three of those modes have means of expressing emotion not available online — tone of voice on the phone, voice and facial cues and body language in person, and flair of script and print in handwritten letters. The last is the weakest emotional indicator of the three, but nonetheless still lacking online. No wonder, then, that the online communicator feels a need to get emotion through the lines of electronic text.

A variety of approaches have developed over the years.

Some folks like to emphasize words like *this*. Others, perhaps a bit more modest in soul, use _this_ approach. And there are those who simply opt for all CAPITALS.

More adventurous still are folks who try to utilize control characters to deliver some special effect like inverse video (white letters on dark background). And the more multi-media oriented have been known to surround their to-be emphasized words in beeps.

And then there is the use of the parenthetical qualifier < smirk > — imported from the hot-chat emotive online jungle of Compuserve (the nation's largest online system). I suppose an occasional < grin >, < laugh >, < chuckle > or < smile > can add spice to otherwise flat or ambiguous text. And given Levinson's addendum to Murphy's Law — whenever a communication is the least bit ambiguous, it will always be understood in a way the author did not intend — a few < smile >'s here and there might stop a reader from taking unintended offense to a dry sarcasm which, if delivered in person with a twinkle in the eye, would amuse rather than anger. Nonetheless, for my tastes these < grin >'s can be easily overused, with the result that the text has the flavor of cheap french fries drowning in ketchup < gag >.

"Emoticons" — emotion icons, as in:

        :-) for a smile,
        :-(for a frown,
        %-) for a smile with eyeglasses,
        :-}) for a smile with a goatee, etc.

— do the same work as the linguistic qualifiers, show a certain style, and thus are easier to take. But if overused they can literally be a pain in the neck — since you have to bend your head sideways to see them — and they run the risk of making your text look like punctuation soup.

Which returns me to the contributor who gave me so much aggro, as they say in England where he resided, several years ago. Maybe he was right that if you have to pump up a word to make its meaning comprehensible, you're using the wrong word. Why not take advantage of the fluidity and multidimensionality of our language, and strive to choose and arrange words in such a way that we understand their import without ketchup? In this, I suspect the problems we encounter in online communication are much like those encountered by writers since the beginning of (recorded) time.

And at the same time there is, as the literary critic I. A. Richards said, a certain value, even beauty, in ambiguity itself. Sometimes it's nice as a reader to be faced with a variety of possible meanings, differing glints and shades you obtain by looking at a word this way and that.

Shakespeare himself was the master both in finding just the right word and in hitting upon what Richards called that "exquisite" ambiguity.

As in the haunting last line of Hamlet —

"And the rest is silence."

No need for a :-(to follow that, now is there....

PERRY MASON RETURNS
TO PLATO'S LAMENT

Perry Mason has returned to our television screens — not in reruns, but in new movie-length episodes, starring the ever portlier Raymond Burr. The best thing about these new episodes is that old music — the compelling signature of big band, '40s hot jazz, with just a touch of Stravinsky discord thrown in that somehow piques your interest every time the predictability of the plot begins lulling you to sleep. Just like in the old days.

Indeed, music has been the driving force behind the TV detective/police/lawyer show from its beginnings in the melodramatic *Dragnet* to its macho adolescence in *Peter Gunn* through the "defective detective" that dominated the genre through the late '60s and most of the '70s.

(I first noticed this defective detective gambit when preparing my Popular Culture and the Media course several years ago: Cannon was overweight; Barnaby Jones over the hill; Ironsides confined to a wheelchair; Longstreet blind; Kojak bald; McCloud a hick; Rockford a bum; Colombo a schlep; and so on ad defectum....)

The 1980s smash *Miami Vice* was really an hour-long music video, in which the thinly woven and often incomprehensible plot was but a vehicle for the exposition of the great music. (*"Miami Vice* is gonna be all Doors tonight," a student excitedly told me a few years ago, referring to the ever-enigmatic and hypnotic Jim Morrison and company. See "Miami Symbiosis" in these Chronicles for more on *Miami Vice*.)

Nor is this prevalence of background music that is really the star limited to TV detective shows. We are often programmed without knowing it to feel romantic, sad, disposed to laughter, love, and anger by the music we encounter in our media. Advertisers know this well, and often spend millions of dollars producing just the right acoustic environments for their 30 second mini-plays.

None of this would surprise Plato, who understood and feared the effect of music on our psyches, and banned poets and musicians both from his ideal Republic. His hubris was that he imagined intellect could function without an emotional matrix — making Plato a strange bedfellow of many current enthusiasts of artificial intelligence, though Plato hadn't much use for machines either. (Of the triumvirate of Socrates, Plato, and Aristotle, only the last had much regard for the tool.)

In *The Open Society and Its Enemies*, Karl Popper — a great lover of music, incidentally, and in my assessment one of the great philosophers of the 20th century — shows how Plato's exaltation of rational intellect to the point of dictatorship provided a spiritual basis for 20th century totalitarianism. So here's our dilemma: music can indeed be a bending of the psyche. We ride in a car, innocently turn on the radio, and are suddenly thrust into a mood conveyed by a song that we happen to associate with a certain period in our lives. The grip of such tunes can include tugs on our patriotism and all manner of deliberate manipulation by people who know how to do such things. And yet the Platonic alternative of controlling music is far worse, for inhibition of any communication, musical or otherwise, risks stifling expression and dissent — a far surer path to loss of freedom than any conceivable musical manipulation.

And so music may indeed be a drug, as Plato says, and Perry Mason a quick sugar kick, but there are worse sources of pleasure in this world, and I'm for legalization all the way, Your Honor.

< Pan out to reveal Plato sitting in Judge's robes, distinguished panel of philosophers including Popper and Bertrand Russell on the jury. Bring in closing theme in crescendo. Fade to public service commercial about the Constitution. >

CHRISTMAS CHRONICLE

The Phil Spector Christmas Album is available in the stores again, after a nearly two decade absence in some areas. It caused quite a stir when first released in 1962, with pulsing "wall-of-sound" rock renditions of such sentimental classics as "I Saw Mommy Kissing Santa Claus." Now the Ronettes' rock version sounds more normal to our ears than the original Jimmy Bowen crooning of 1952, so accustomed have we become to the 40 year hegemony of rock 'n' roll.

Religion has always been intimately intertwined with entertainment and flashy media. The alphabet, a quick moving radical departure from wallpaper hieroglyphics, helped pave the way for monotheism by giving people the ability to write and read about an all-powerful, all-present, invisible Deity (not easy to draw a picture of such an entity). Similarly the Bible — the online seminar of its day (multiple "notes" of varying length and style "entered" by varied witnesses) — became and continues to be a bedrock of Western religion. (The Hebrew Talmud is an especially significant precursor in both structure and literal appearance to an online discussion, consisting of more than a millennium of comments upon comments upon comments.)

The mere survival of any medium, let alone its service as a vessel of religion, tends to imbue it with a certain dignity and even grounds for reverence. Similarly, we tend to scoff at new media and the roles they might play, even are currently playing, in profound human activities like affairs of the spirit. Music is a suitable companion of faith as long as the strains are classical or at least circa 1940s old; rock 'n' roll is suspect in many places. The engraved texts of the Torah, Bible, and Koran are sacred; but who'd expect to find much of anything other than the mildly sacrilegious in an online database?

Well, believe it or not, there are already very interesting — I would even say profound — interminglings of electronic data and religion going on in several areas. These range from Bibles on computer disks, to online courses in religion, to even an "electronic" chapel. You access this "place" as you would any database, but once you enter, you find an environment that's quite different. A random continuing stream of inspirations greets you, culled from the great religions of the past and present. After reading as many of these as you wish, you are free to enter your own inspiration, and/or a commentary on the experience you've just had. These in turn become part of the canon, to be read by others.*

My religious views — which tend to run in the naturalistic deity-in-humans mode of Emerson (with my own technological twist thrown in) — differ from the established "place"-based religions. But even were I a devout member of some traditional religion, I think I would still pay serious attention to the possibilities for communion of spirit in the new winged-word medium of computers. Spirit was and is after all communicated via symbols, and electronic text excels in the give and take of symbols like no other.

"Electricity has made angels of us all," Edmund Carpenter (anthropologist and colleague of McLuhan) wrote years ago in *Oh, What a Blow That Phantom Gave Me!* He was talking not about the ethical, but the metaphysical qualities of angels, though perhaps the two have more than a coincidental connection. Heretofore only denizens of heaven could be in more than one place at the same time. Now, via electricity, so can we.

---

*January, 1992: This electronic chapel was designed by Peter and Trudy Johnson-Lenz. It was called "Attune," and was situated on the Electronic Information Exchange System (the home network for Connected Education, 1985-1991). When EIES went offline in 1991, so too, alas, did Attune.

THE CURSOR AND THE MOON

I began teaching this online term with the splash of seaweed and the smell of salt on sultry Cape Cod bay in August. Fitting, then, that I should conclude the term again on the Cape, with the cool lucid stars of December 31st shining through my window as I write this.

It's hard for a city boy like me to leave the metropolis and its wonders, and I'd given some thought lately to why Tina and my family and I so enjoy these sojourns into peace and quietude. I've always prided myself on hating vacations — holidays always seemed to me devices of the establishment to maintain the status quo a little longer by slowing down the pace of life a bit. I like fresh air all right, but I dislike doing nothing.

And yet now I think we would move up here permanently if we could. What has come over me?

Our online network. Computer conferencing in general, but our online system in particular, seems like a city to me. Always open, with better conversation than found in the restaurants of New York. Multiple ways of doing the same thing (just like taxis, buses, automobiles, etc. in the city, we have at least three ways of copying conference comments and messages on our system). An image of many simultaneous independent modules of life and intelligence comes to my mind when I picture either the city or our online network as a whole.

But I can access this new network-city in the country, with the waves and the stars in my face. I'm able to leave the physical city only because I carry the informational city in the four pounds of TRS 80 M100 computer and equipment in my briefcase.

Of course, the informational city has its limits. Conversation may be better and more plentiful than in traditional restaurants, food for thought may be top quality, but food for eating is non-existent. For such food, indeed for all pleasures and matters of physical presence, the online denizen must embrace the offline world. And here the peace and beauty of the country may not satisfy in every respect what Samuel Johnson had in mind when he said that one who tires of London tires of life itself.

Still, a large part of what Johnson was talking about was stimulation of the intellect, a resource in which online life abounds. In the end, the best that we humans can do is increase our choices. If we can enjoy the intellect of the city and the breeze of the country, but not the food of the city restaurant, we're still better off than in the old days when the intellect of the city was available only in the city, with no sweet breeze, and whether we wanted the restaurant or not.

So now we have intellect in two places — which is to say, because one of the places is online, in all places — and the seafood on Cape Cod, not to mention the Italian cuisine, is every bit as delicious as that in New York.

So tonight we'll watch the ball drop all right — two in fact — the cursor and the moon.

HAVIN' A PARTI

Most users of online systems know about their own system, but little about others. Part of this reflects what I call the "first-love syndrome," in which users fall in love with the first online system on which they become comfortable, and are therefore resistant to the benefits of other online systems. We here on the Electronic Information Exchange System (EIES) are by no means immune to this,* and so I thought I'd tell you a bit about an offshoot of EIES that went its own way and has developed into quite a sophisticated computer conferencing system.

Several years ago, a group of EIES users including Harry Stevens (who was involved in Cambridge politics in the 1960s) and Peter and Trudy Johnson-Lenz (who later went on to develop the MIST and MIST+ micro software systems) began work here on EIES on a sub-system called "Topics." This was a new approach to conferencing that entailed something called "branching." As Harry later told me, when the new approach was sufficiently different from the original EIES design, a group of the branch-workers decided to take this new software and market it commercially. (The New Jersey Institute of Technology — the owner of EIES — was not interested in commercial marketing, since it received the lion's share of its capital for online systems development from government grants.) The result was the Participate or Parti system, the highly popular computer conferencing module of the Source (until sold to CompuServe in the summer of 1989), and still going strong on several networks in the US, and in such places as Toronto, Paris, and Tokyo.**

In April of 1985, I conducted an "Electure" on Parti on the Source called "Space: Humanizing the Universe." More than 450 participants entered some 1,000 comments in a month's time, and I learned a lot about Parti in those exciting days.

I found Parti to have three important advantages over most other online systems:

1. Users can set up multiple identities on single accounts on Parti. For example, on Parti, I could have the identity Director

(for Director of Connected Education), Prof. Paul Levinson (for my teaching and commentator work — as in this conference) and Paul Levinson (for personal online work). When not abused by usage designed to deceive, these multiple identities can give readers a clearer understanding of what you are doing online.

2. People can form new conferences or topics on Parti with the ease that people send private messages on other systems. In other words, I could set up a private conference or topic with every person with whom I was conversing, either instead or of in addition to an exchange of private messages. Whether for the conducting of private tutorials or long business conversations, such a system is very helpful.

3. Branching allows members of a conference to start new attached conferences — "branches" — when entering comments in the original conference. For example, if these Chronicles were on Parti, I might enter the present comment as a special "opener" comment to a new branch devoted to discussion of Parti. Other branches could be opened for discussion of other themes raised in the Chronicles, allowing for a neat structural organization of comments.

Have a look at the "branch map" of my "Space" Electure on Parti:

"SPACE" by CONNECTED EDUCATION, Apr. 12, 1985 at 23:12 about HUMANIZING THE UNIVERSE ... A NEW ELECTURE BY DR. PAUL LEVINSON ... WITH LISA CARLSON SPACE GUIDE (27 notes)

> 4: "SPACE TALK" (555 notes)
>> 122: "FUTURE WORLD" (33 notes)
>> 123: "SPACE STUFF" (16 notes)
>> 124: "CRITICAL STAGE" (16 notes)
>> 467: "SPACE ACTIVISTS" (25 notes)
>> 468: "SPACE AND SPIRIT" (48 notes)
>>> 48: "HYMN FOR SPACEFARERS" (3 notes)
> 5: "SPACE THE TV SERIES" (24 notes)
> 6: "SPACE DEFENSE" (206 notes)
> 7: "SPACE RORSCHACH" (11 notes)

8: "SPACE BEINGS" (169 notes)
9: "SPACE MEDIA" (7 notes)
10: "SPACE INDEX" (4 notes)
11: "SPACE GUESTS" (9 notes)
18: "SPACE TAX" (40 notes)

As you can see, the general conference "Space" (in which only I and Parti Assistant Lisa Carlson could enter comments), contains but 27 comments. Of these, nine were "openers" or the beginning of new subconferences or branches (Space Talk, Space the TV Series, Space Defense, Space Rorshach, Space Beings, Space Media, Space Guests, Space Tax created by me; Space Index by Lisa). Listed in parentheses are the number of comments generated in each branch (so Space Talk, which begins as its own branch in the 4th comment in Space, generated 555 comments or notes of its own). Further, Space Talk — which was set up as the primary interactive branch, or place where participants could enter their own comments (and even start their own branches) — itself was the parent of five sub-subconferences or branches of branches (Critical Stage, Space Activists, and Space Spirit, the products of science fiction author Sylvia Engdahl, who joined as an unexpected much welcome participant, and has since gone on to become Special Projects assistant for Connected Education and part of the Connect Ed online faculty). Finally, Sylvia even added a sub-sub-subconference with her "Hymn" (to the Challenger), entered some eight months after conclusion of the formal Electure. (The 27th comment or note in the main Space Conference was similarly entered by me well after the conclusion of the Electure in memoriam to the Challenger. It appears here in these Chronicles as "Interrupted Journey.")

A big advantage of this structure is that it gives an excellent map or table of contents of what would otherwise be more than 1,000 comments entered in simple linear fashion. This is clearly a necessity when dealing with large numbers of active participants.

One *dis*advantage is that branching can sometimes result in fragmentation of a conference, when participants start branches for virtually every thought that comes to mind. The result is that the reader is unsure where to look for discussion of a specific theme in a multitude of branches with similar titles.

Of course, a conference group or moderator can always elect not to use branching where available, either by agreement or by restricting the user's options.

Ultimately, my assessment of online systems is much like my philosophy of technology and human choice: systems that increase one's options are in general better than systems that do not. The heightening of noise and possibility for error that comes with options is more than compensated for by the fine tuning such options provide for the conduct of our business and lives.

---

*January, 1992: Indeed, Connect Ed stayed on EIES almost to the bitter end, moving to the Participate system on Unison in August, 1991, about three months before EIES went offline.

**January, 1992: As indicated in the above note, Connect Ed is now situated on Participate on Unison, with the largest number of online students in three years. CompuServe currently has a Participate system — "The Point" — though the Point has a much lower profile relative to CompuServe than the old Parti system did to the Source.

ABCs OF ONLINE EDUCATION

The ideal of universal education has long been associated with democratic and humanistic principles. In the Renaissance and early modern times especially, theorists such as John Locke and J. A. Comenius saw the extension of education beyond the aristocracy (Comenius specifically urged the education of young women) as crucial to development and maintenance of the human spirit on a personal level, and the wellbeing of society as a whole.

Interestingly, both theorists viewed the human mind as a "blank slate," malleable and to be written upon by the enlightened educator. For Comenius, the student's mind was like "paper … to be imprinted with the symbols of knowledge" (*The Great Didactic*). And Locke, well known for his "tabula rasa" concept of human mentality in general, readily applied this perspective to education.

Comenius' print metaphor was well-suited to the dominant medium of his time: through books, one lecture or discourse could indeed be dispersed universally (though until the reduction in cost of printing brought about by technological improvements in the mid-19th century, the cost of an average book — equal to an average workingman's monthly salary in in the U.S. in 1800, for example — kept it from anything remotely like universality). And the development of electronic mass media in the 20th century greatly broadened the possibilities for universal "imprinting" of symbols of knowledge.

And yet, as all of us know, mere dissemination of information via books and mass media alone does not constitute education. There is an interactive quality — a give and take between the student and teacher — that seems essential if both parties are to grow and benefit from the exchange. As Henry Perkinson points out in his "Education and Learning from Our Mistakes" (in *In Pursuit of Truth*, ed. Paul Levinson, Humanities Press, 1982, pp. 126-153), modern educational theorists from Montessori to Piaget have recognized that learning is an intrinsically active process, much more of a reaching out and digesting and altering of the instruction (and instructor) than a receipt of symbols by a passive, bucket mind.

Since, as Socrates pointed out, books are unresponsive to questions of readers, mass media even at their best are not adequate to the task of interactive education. Clearly online education is. (Neil Postman misses this point in his constant critique of TV and lauding of print, e.g., *Amusing Ourselves to Death*, 1985. From the interactive standpoint — or lack of — the book is far closer to TV than it is to computer conferencing.)

Thus, we might say that, in principle, online education provides the best hope of universal education, for it combines global dispersement of information with interactive capacity. (See my "Social Dimensions of OnLine Communities" in these Chronicles for more on the interactive quality of online communication vs. books in education.)

But realization of principles requires something more — in the case of education, it requires a special kind of teacher. A successful online teacher must be both an adept writer and a sensitive teacher. Yet in the traditional educational institution, good writers and good in-class teachers are rarely found in the same person, and indeed departments often split into two distinct groups along these lines.

The online teacher, then, will be both an unusual and unifying person.

TAKING CARE OF BUSINESS

Did you know that...

• A major American corporation has been using an online network for more than a decade, but they do their best to keep this activity strictly secret. They think online communication gives them a competitive edge over their rivals that they'd rather not publicize.

• Another corporation instituted online communication in its organization, and then abruptly withdrew it after several months. The reason: Upper-middle level management felt that access to online discussions by underlings weakened the supervisors' position of authority.

As sociologist Erving Goffman (and more recently media theorist Joshua Meyrowitz, *No Sense of Place*, 1985) have emphasized, hierarchies based on differing access to information (and thus power) are what make business (and society as a whole) tick. Used in a non-thoughtful way, online communication can jeopardize those hierarchies by making information too available to too many, thus upsetting the corporate applecart (this is what happened in our second case). Even when used carefully, online communication is a natural hierarchy-buster: the boss sitting behind a big desk in a plush office is missing in an online message that this same boss sends to underlings online.

What can done?

Well, online design can encourage control of information in ways that wherever possible support rather than undermine traditional hierarchies of power. Making particular people read-only members of topics, giving supervisors and executives the power to "tailor" discussions (decide the amount of time that a note will be available online, limit the length of notes for various members of the online group), etc. would shore up hierarchies in this regard.

But what if levelling of hierarchies is for the better? Perhaps a more equal playing field in corporate teams can result in improved performance.

If such is the case, then the best corporate policy regarding online communication is go with the flow — that is, allow the new availability of information via online systems to sweep aside or alter traditional structures. Greater exposure to information could encourage greater constructive participation of all people on the offline corporate ladder, with commensurate increases in useful criticism, creativity (as more creators gain exposure), and a general unleashing and focusing of productive energy.

These two approaches — molding of online systems to traditional corporate needs, molding of corporate America to more informationally-equal access — are in fact both being tried and espoused by varieties of companies, and are the subject of considerable behind the scenes debate.

Nor are these two approaches mutually exclusive — both can easily be accommodated on most online systems. But in making a decision about which approach to go with in a given project, corporate managers and execs would do well to remember George Bernard Shaw's observation that reasonable people adapt to their surroundings, unreasonable people strive to adapt their surroundings to themselves, and all progress depends upon unreasonable people. In that sense, the "unreason" of online communication may be its greatest asset for business.

SEEING EDWARD R. MURROW NOW

HBO's original (made for HBO) movies have generally been a mixed lot, long on big stars and international locations, short on worthwhile or even interesting story lines. Their Sakharov movie was a sparkling exception, and their movie on Murrow, which I saw again last week, was another gem.

Murrow in reality was a strange, almost paradoxical person. Shy, uncomfortable, sometimes nearly bending backwards in front of the TV camera, he used this vehicle to address Americans directly on some of the most wrenching issues of the 1950s, such as his forthright attack on the un-American activities of Joseph McCarthy.

Television, he tells CBS-TV head William Paley, has the ability to really make a difference in public life if used correctly. Paley believes Murrow in his heart of hearts, but succumbs to the pressures of chasing the big dollar via sitcoms and quizshows.

Murrow's optimism on first inspection seems well founded. After all, TV and radio are available to everyone — no one has to learn to use these media that populate our homes like so much wallpaper — and thus quality material sent via these conveyors should have maximum penetration of the public. What easier way is there of appealing to people's best tastes?

But perhaps the ease of TV is precisely why best tastes are so difficult to stimulate via this medium. Maybe in a structure that allows events to come to us so effortlessly, all we're willing to accept are events in their simplest, cartoon character presentation.

Online discourse via personal computers and modems is of course much more painfully attained, especially when the would-be attainers are adults. Skills are always more difficult to master after childhood, and for most of us, driving a car is about the last major skill we expect to sweat for and acquire.

Then these glowing phosphor screens come along, hooked up to what looks a lot like a typewriter but works like a wand (whose mastery requires learning of something akin to a foreign language), and having some further unfathomable connection to the telephone that we're accustomed to simply talk through, and ... let's face it, acquiring any sort of skill with the personally teleconnected computer is far from easy, and no one wants to become a child again at the behest of learning how to do this. Certainly even the easiest computer use is much more difficult than turning on a television — just press a button, lean back, half close your eyes, and let the pictures roll by.

And so computer designers work round the clock to ease our interface and uncrease our face, developing user-friendly software, front-end software, rear-end software, hardware of all sorts and medium-boiled ware, and even so, we still find it hard to get on top of the computer. It's so unforgiving — a colon rather than a semi-colon during sign-on can sink you.

And yet perhaps this painful on-lining has a silver lining, perhaps the very difficulty with which mastery of this medium is achieved will oblige at least this — we — the first generation of online users to treat what we read and write here more seriously.

A science fiction writer at heart, I always like to play the game of what if — what if Edward R. Murrow had been an electronic journalist who used the medium of glowing printed words rather than speech or speech and images? We already have a few online journalists — like Mike Greenly, whose reportage on AIDS is among the most vivid in this area — and I suspect this medium will lend itself well to the finest of reporting in the future. (See my "Chronicle of AIDS" in these Chronicles for more on Greenly's work.)

Will commercial interests ultimately take over our online communities as they did at CBS-TV? "This topic brought to you by Brand X Disk Cleaner..."*

Not that commercial sponsorship of mass media is bad — it's certainly preferable to the government control found in most other societies, and is likely the best way of supporting and even controlling our one-way mass media environment.

But we may be creating something different here online, for along with the high costs and frustrations of learning to use this medium come a very entrenched decentralization and individual power which will be hard to shortcircuit.

We and our online colleagues may be developing a medium in which Edward R. Murrow would've been very comfortable.

---

*January, 1992: The IBM-Sears "Prodigy" online system does now have a large amount of online advertising attached to topics and texts. Prodigy has also been the subject of some controversy regarding what its users claim to be attempts to censor their online communication. To what extent these two factors are related — commercial sponsorship and eroding of the sense of decentralization and individual control heretofore the hallmark of online communication — is a question worthy of further investigation.

INTERRUPTED JOURNEY:
JANUARY 28, 1986

The wrenching image of today's Space Shuttle tragedy surely ranks with the assassinations of the '60s, the explosion of the Hindenburg, and some of the worst visions in our cultural history. The heartbreak of students in New Hampshire watching their teacher on the screen, the symbol of the cross section of Americans going up in flame, will not soon be forgotten by people in this country or humans anywhere on the planet.

We must be careful not to jump to wrong, even perverse conclusions from this awful event. There is a strong, understandable feeling, an anger, that the space program isn't worth the toll in human life — that we ought at very least to send robots and machines, not vulnerable human lives on our exploits into space. Yet such conclusions would run contrary to the dreams of those people on their way to space, who knew that artificial intelligences are not substitutes for the qualities of hope and wonder and inspiration that humans carry with them in encounters with the cosmos.

We are reminded again of the inescapable imperfection of our technologies. We expect too much of them, and no amount of checking and double checking and safety precautions can ever be enough. Yet what else can we do? The temptation to damn fire because it accidentally kills is powerful indeed, yet without fire we all would die a slow death anyway.

The denizens of the future who today gave their lives understood this better than most people — that a human future without space development would be a confined and ultimately suffocating future for Earth-bound humanity. Their optimism in taking part in such a venture was not a blind optimism, but a faith born of knowing that there is no other way for humanity, other than up and out to the stars.

We with tears in our eyes now must make sure that this faith in the future is not a further casualty of today's toll. We owe it to these brave voyagers to find out what went wrong, do our utmost to make sure it does not happen again, and then resume where this journey left off....

PRESCRIBING A VIDEO PRESIDENCY

The death of the Challenger astronauts has got me thinking again about the necessity of exposing human lives to risk in the pursuit of public tasks in this our information age. As I indicated in my response to the space tragedy, I see human space travellers as crucial to our expansion into space — only humans at this point in our robotics and AI knowledge are capable of dealing with surprise. I suspect that if and when we develop AI machines that have similar capacities to deal with the unexpected, they may well qualify for status as living beings.

But physical presence may not be so crucial in other dangerous, Earth-bound tasks. Consider the President, presumably elected for his or her abilities of wisdom and leadership, not personal appearances and handshaking.

Yet the personal appearance — the pre-campaign trip, the AFL-CIO talk — has in my lifetime taken the lives of one of our Presidents (JFK) and nearly taken the life of another (Reagan). Or rather, such personal appearances have put every recent president's life at risk, with tragic and near-tragic result in the above two cases.

What purpose do such appearances serve in a world in which appearance can be made even more effectively and intimately in many ways via video? Cannot a talk to a convention be given more dramatically via video, through which all watchers can see close-ups of the speaker in the comfort of their homes (as in an online convention) or even a hotel room?

In-person contact has its undeniable charms, and certainly its replacement via video or other remote means would utterly miss the point in some cases. Irreplaceable in-person situations that come to mind are making love, swimming in the ocean, or dining in a fine restaurant — and viva the irreplaceability in these and like cases.

But are the duties of a President similarly in-person bound? Surely, the essence of leadership is decision-making and promotion of decisions once made, and surely these tasks are primarily information not flesh oriented.

I know, I know. Mention of a "video presidency" brings to mind a *1984*-like facade of leadership, a *Star Trek* episode in which the leader of some world is really a TV prop for some evil behind-the-scenes manipulator.

No solution or set of precautions is perfect. But then, neither is standing pat. We now live in world in which presidents and other important people can be hunted by diabolic weapons of death. Is the best proof we can muster against this the antiquated personal bodyguard of the Secret Service? At least twice in our recent history, the bodyguard approach was much too late.

Disasters such as the Challenger's are in principle impossible to ever completely guard against, because they involve technologies which are in themselves extensions into the unknown.

But in the case of safeguarding the consequences of our elections from exposure to destruction, we have the ability to be more pro-active. We can take steps to drastically reduce the mania for personal appearances and in-person campaigning of our presidents that continually puts them at mortal risk, and instead be content to watch their images on the screens.

It'll be either that, or, I'm afraid, another round of national grief sooner or later.

MEDIATED GRIEF

Shock and grief about the loss of people we do not know is not entirely a consequence of our electronic age. Humans for eons have after all mourned the loss of their kings, queens, and popular heroes, and most of this occurred in a time before TV and for that matter even a press. Still, the electronic nervous system to which we all are in one way or another now connected has given a new type of prominence and vividness to public grief.

As Joshua Meyrowitz points out in his *No Sense of Place* (Oxford, 1985), one element of this new emotion arises when we lose a person we have come to know as a media intimate through television, radio, and recordings. John Lennon knew but a tiny fraction of the millions who listened to his voice alone in the dark — but most of these millions felt that Lennon was singing personally to them, and they mourned his death as intensely as they would a close friend's, teacher's, or even relative's or lover's. Coleridge tells us that poetic faith is grounded in a willing suspension of disbelief, and this suspension extends not only to the appreciation of music and art, but to the relationships we create with our remote artists. For the same reasons, we feel we know political leaders and others in the media too on this level, and the killings of the Kennedys and Martin Luther King in the '60s were thus as much poetic as political in their effect, and the wound acutely personal.

The Challenger disaster was actually a bit different. Here we didn't know the victims very well (if at all) beforehand, but via the media we came to be eyewitnesses to their death. (An ironic parallel of the Shuttle explosion is the killing of Lee Harvey Oswald — also witnessed by gasping viewers on the Evening News — though in Oswald's case the loss was of a presumed villain rather than a group of undeniable heroes.) Having come to know these people in so intense, direct, and profound a way — witnessing their deaths — we suddenly have an unrequiting need to know everything else we can know about them, a need which the media also fulfill. And so the astronauts become members of our families retroactively, intimates of ours in retrospect, and the cycle of mediated grief proceeds.

The newest and as yet unpredictable piece of this communications pattern is the advent of electronic interactive-public media such as online systems. Those few of us fortunate to have entree to this vehicle need no longer be balloons that can only receive and be filled with the sadness we get from broadcast media. We can, in addition to talking to our in-person families and circles, now express our responses in the more public forum of online networks. We can add our touch to the mosaic of public mourning, and the comments I've seen here in our own Connect Ed online conferences, as well as elsewhere on other networks such as The Source, are among the most sensitive and penetrating I've come across on the tragic Challenger explosion.

The problem is that this interactive link is still so very tiny compared to the ocean-size window of mass electronic media. I long for the day that this interactive capacity will make its contribution to all people's views of themselves and our planet and its heroes.

WHEN ONE VCR JUST ISN'T ENOUGH

Hot night on television last night. Three attractive programs up against each other: *The Fifth Missile* on NBC, *Blood and Orchids* on CBS, and *Crossings* on ABC. Not the highest quality of entertainment ever available, but you can't have the caviar of online networking every night.

The fact is, my family and I would've enjoyed watching each of the three. But the networks, putting them back to back, made this impossible and thrust upon our household the awful burden of TV decision. Only a home with two VCRs could have transcended the dilemma, and alas we have but one.

My vote was for *The Fifth Missile*. I like these military tension, world-in-peril dramas, and besides I thought the strategic connotations of this Trident sub-gone-insane movie might give me some valuable pointers for my work in ethics of technology.

My wife wanted *Blood and Orchids*. She claimed it was the classiest of the three dramas, but I think she really wanted to get a chance to look at Kris Kristofferson for a few hours.

Crossings was everyone's second choice. Anything other than an end-of-world melodrama was preferable for my wife, and Jane Seymour and Cheryl Ladd gave this mini-series good marks in my book.

Television is often said to shamelessly pander to the public's desires. But how is public desire pandered to by presenting the public with a trilemma — a double no-win situation in which we are bound to be disappointed twice as much as we are pleased?

February is sweep month on TV, a time when the networks throw everything they have into the quest for ratings. Ongoing series offer their best stuff (*Hill Street Blues* had Furillo almost killed; *St. Elsewhere* had a marvelous two-part historical of 50 years of the hospital with actors playing hilarious and touching younger dramatic selves), and mini-series pop up virtually every weekend. Apparently, though, the networks have never heard of game theory (game shows, yes — but not game theory): and so they are prone to program themselves into a lose/lose situation by putting blockbusters in head-to-head competition, rather than guaranteeing some audience — a win/win approach — by staggering their special programs.

NBC seems to be the most sensible of the three. Heady a few months ago with the success of their *Miami Vice* — an hour-long video or vehicle for the exhibition of great music starring sets of chic clothes — they thought to take the ultimate challenge and move this show up against CBS' *Dallas* (presumably weakened by the loss of Bobby Ewing at the end of last year). But *Dallas* has apparently been strengthened by Bobby's loss (he was a nebbish anyway [nebbish is Yiddish for wimp, for the non-cognoscenti], and *Miami* began fading in its 9-10 PM spot. NBC quickly realized its error, and they restored *Miami* to its safer 10-11 PM spot, where it's now recuperating nicely.

Indeed, programming the one-shot *Fifth Missile* against tawdry sexy mini-series was probably the most intelligent move of the three. Those with a hunger for illicit romance would be split between the two mini-series, with the *Missile* movie torpedoing whatever remaining chance either CBS or ABC had for victory in the weekend, thus further sinking their campaigns to catch the first place NBC....

Gee, I wonder if anyone has studied what effect watching TV has on one's propensity for forced metaphor.

MANILA AND STOCKHOLM:
THE UNMEDIATED SOCIETY

A pleasant surprise in Manila, and that old agonizing wound again in Stockholm this week. A dictator bows to democracy in the Philippines, and in Sweden a man of peace is gunned down — both intensely human stories, but both highlighting the peculiar roles of media in our world.

Media have their limits. In the hands of a dictator, media can be powerful tools for keeping democracy down. As portrayed in Orwell's obsolete but instructive *1984*, media in their extreme can even deprive us of the language needed to think freely. In real life, they can certainly get in the way of the democratic impulse.

But not stop it totally. Marcos controlled most of the means of communication in the Philippines, but not all of them, and this itself is a limitation on anyone who seeks to totally control society through control of information. Given even a ray of light by which to see reason, people just won't buy an election return of 14 million to the victor and 0 to the opponent. A car without a driver doesn't move, and a medium without watchers has no effect. So media and their controllers are dependent upon their watchers, and every once in a while the watchers rise up and object to what they are shown. In a phrase, media can only be as powerful as people let them be, and in the Philippines people demonstrated just who holds the ultimate power in this relationship. Doesn't happen very often, but it's quite salutary when it does.

Media also are involved in limitations of a different sort. They limit the physical exposure of leaders to their people — supplying instead the image and the representation, the information of decision rather than the physical presence of decision-maker him or herself. (See my chronicle "Prescribing a Video Presidency" for more.)

Some critics see this function of media as counter-democratic, but I see it as one of the best tools on behalf of democracy. For the unmediated democratic leader — the person who walks in the streets and guides a nation — runs the risk of succumbing to the profoundest of undemocratic forces: the bullet shot by a lunatic or a lunatic political fringe.

Olaf Palme was a man of peace — a Martin Luther King of the international arena, who was courageous in his condemnations of both West and East when they pursued policies that were morally questionable and strategically hazardous. His vision of the world was a refinement of modern Swedish thought: that reason and dialogue must temper our taste for anger and violence.

But this vision was no defense against the bullets that gunned him down, for ideas however right and wonderful are never a match for steel in the immediate sense. Assassins understand bullet proof vests and tight security, not philosophies that show the stupidity and eventual futility of violence.

And the tightest security is rarely appearing in public at all. This is a bitter sacrifice for people like Palme — and Martin Luther King, and Robert Kennedy, and John Kennedy — who love people, but is loss of life any less a sacrifice? And which poses the greatest threat to democracy: a more cloistered leadership, or a leadership vulnerable to the whims of any warped person with a gun, or any perverted political group, that comes along?

Gentle people like Palme deserve better than dying in a pool of blood on a public street. They deserve better than satisfying the sick desires of those who seek destiny, a cheap touch of greatness, by slaughtering the great.

They deserve all the logic and protection that our information society can give ... and if this means a more personally remote leadership, then so be it.

THE TRIAL OF NASA

When I first started these Chronicles I had in the back of my mind an idea about alternating more serious discussions with pop culture criticism, humor, and lighter topics. Events in the last two months especially have made this game plan difficult to follow. Perhaps the plan was unrealistic to start with.

The past week has brought the Challenger explosion to the fore of our attention again — it never was really too far below it —with reports of engineers advising against the launch and being pressured by management to ok it, astronauts indicating their general lack of trust in NASA and the Space Shuttle, and an increasing condemnation of NASA's handling of humans in space from a variety of quarters. This snowballing televised series of alleged and apparently documented wrongdoings reminds me of the Watergate hearings — and I fear the result may be as destructive to the space program as Watergate was to the then President.

But would such results be as warranted? Aside from the distinction between NASA in particular and the space program in general (we can oppose one and support the other), I think that we ought to bear several things in mind when considering the role and performance of NASA in the Challenger disaster.

One is that failure tends to ratify and reinforce doubters and sceptics, just as success reinforces everyone who is optimistic about a venture. Without having any direct knowledge about the recommendations that NASA decision-makers were subject to on all previous missions, I'd guess that every mission must have had, somewhere along the line, those who expressed concern about this or that component or operation. And the success of those missions had to weaken the attention NASA paid to these concerns in future missions, and strengthen the counsel of those who advised to proceed in spite of possible problems. Such a development, I think, is not a question of irresponsibility on NASA's or anyone's part, but an all but irresistible fact of human social dynamics.

The same dynamic works in reverse when a dramatic failure occurs. In the aftermath of the Challenger tragedy, anyone who had even the slightest qualm about the Challenger or any shuttle mission suddenly has these qualms vividly corroborated. The impression given is that a NASA bent on pleasing the President blithely ignored an avalanche of well-framed and clear-cut counter-indications to launch, but the reality more likely is that many of these doubts became clearcut *after* the horrible explosion over Florida, when malfunction and death provided awful expression and completion to partly formed equations of doubt. Again, such retrospective surety about initially unclear concerns seems to be an unavoidable facet of social reality, and I intend no criticism of the doubters here in making this observation.

We also suffer, all of us, from a pressing need to find some sort of clean, identifiable reason for the tragedies that befall us personally and as groups and as a species. Given the fact that the Challenger launch killed seven fine people, and that one or more humans were responsible for the go-ahead to launch, ascription of blame of some sort will not be much of a problem. But surely we would do ourselves a service if we went beyond such ascription, beyond the immediate set of pressures — social as well as technical — in which NASA operated, and considered the longer and deeper threads of environment in which NASA and all technological operations must function.

These threads tell us that any technological endeavor is risky, in that new inventions by definition seek to extend our capacities into unknown or little known domains. They tell us that therefore every technological activity will likely have its support- ers and doubters, and that people charged with deciding whether or not to proceed will likely have to ignore some body of advice every time.

We can agree in the Challenger aftermath that cautions ought be given more attention, much more attention, from now on. But we need also be aware that attention to doubt to the extent of stopping a mission could well lead to a situation in which we have no missions at all. Indeed, we would likely still be on the pad with

Sputnik and Explorer had not decision-makers opted to ignore at least some cautionary advisements.

The loss of seven human lives is a horrible price to pay for human settlement of the stars, and steps must be taken to reduce the possibility of this ever happening again. But reduction of this possibility to zero would entail the ending of the entire program of humans in space, thereby rendering the sacrifice of the Challenger astronauts a sacrifice in vain, and the consequence to our species of this development would be even more unacceptable.

We ought to take care, in our trial of NASA, not to foster an environment so punishing of risk and rewarding of doubt that the ending of a space program with human accompaniment is the sterile result.

ROCK 'N' ROLL VS. THE ARBITERS
OF DECENCY

Rock 'n' roll is under attack again. Actually, there've been few times in the 40 year history of this music when it hasn't drawn some sort of dire criticism from the establishment — something in the beat and the words seem to bring out the worst in authority.

As early as 1956, a group of reverends, priests, and rabbis concluded that rock 'n' roll was dangerous to the spiritual and physical well-being of the nation's youth (the report of their finding exists still on a front page of *The New York Times* of that year). In the days before drug usage became the main (not unreasonable) fear that parents had for their children, the sexuality of rock music sent shivers of concern (and likely repressed pleasure) into the lives of fathers and mothers, who sometimes talked as if mere listening to a rock 'n' roll record could make their daughters pregnant.

The persecution of rock music in the 1950s climaxed with the "Payola" scandal of 1959. Here the government sought to crack down on the nefarious practice of DJs playing records for pay (in the form of money, drugs, and women) rather than on the supposedly beneficial standard of whether they liked the record's sound. The victim of payola was presumably the public — though as far as I know, no empirical or aesthetic research ever demonstrated that records played for pay were artistically inferior to records played according to DJ taste. In the end, the main victims of the payola scandal were Alan Freed and other disk jockeys who, while apparently accepting a few bucks under the table now and then, also were responsible for the rise of rock 'n' roll itself in the '50s. In the eyes of the government, this was always their main crime in any case.

The 1960s saw a new twist added to what government agencies thought rock music capable of: towards the end of the decade, the FCC sent a letter to all radio stations advising them they could be held responsible (at license renewal time) for any records they aired which glorified drug usage. Unable to stop the flow of drugs at their international sources, unwilling to do much about the social conditions that engendered drug use in America, the Nixon administration opted for bearing down on the drug problem in the U.S. by pressuring radio stations not to play certain kinds of records.

The main consequences of this crusade? Records that *attacked* drug usage, like Phil Ochs' "Small Circle of Friends" and The Temptations' "Cloud Nine," lost substantial airplay as stations shied away from any mention of drugs in music whatsoever. In any event, songs like Dylan's "Mr. Tambourine Man" ("Take me for a trip upon your magic sailing ship ... My senses have been stripped...") were comprehensible as drug-related only by those already steeped in the drug subculture. Even today, most people would likely think Dylan was singing about a cruise on the Love Boat. Faced with barrages of protests from record companies and some radio stations, the FCC withdrew its drug letter.

And lately, rock 'n' roll is once again under government — or quasi-government — jaundiced scrutiny. The mixture of sexual, commercial, and religious symbolism in rock stars like Madonna and the blunt ghetto language of even brasher "rap" groups make parents and officials angry, and in Washington a group of Senators' wives and other expert parties led by Tipper Gore (wife of the Senator, no relation to Lesley) have managed with varying success to get record releases "rated" beforehand as to their sexual content, etc. The idea is that albums should have ratings much as do movies, even though most observers agree that the "R" rating in movies tends more than anything else to increase box office interest.

So record companies have already begun to voluntarily post ratings on their album covers, but this may not be enough to satisfy Gore et al.'s distaste for audio gore. Music videos — the first really original content of television (the rest is borrowed from film, theater, and radio) — are next in line for some sort of stamp of approval, and the beat of concern about the dangerous effect rock may be having on our nation's children blithely goes on.

AN EASTER THEORY OF TECHNOLOGY

Perhaps the most important question in the history and philosophy of technology is: what circumstances have conspired to turn the seeds of invention, scattered and plentiful throughout history, into the highly technical culture of Western Europe and by extension our present world? Notice that the question is not what makes invention possible — for while marvelous and essential, invention is commonplace — but rather what circumstances are needed to turn brilliant inventions into workaday useable devices. The rarity of advanced technological societies — ours in the West is unique in history — suggests that factors supportive of technological growth may often be hidden and hard to come by.

Major candidates for supportive factors necessary for technological growth are the presence of collateral technologies (e.g., McLuhan's view that the alphabet was prerequisite to success of print in the West; Burlingame's explanation of the failure to actualize Leonardo's inventions as an absence of supportive technologies), the uniquely invigorating climate of free enterprise (von Hayek), and even appropriate physical characteristics in the natural environment (von Hagen's claim that the steep landscape of Mexico foiled Aztec use of the wheel for anything more than toys). While agreeing with all of these fascinating hypotheses, I've always yearned to identify even deeper possible catalysts of Western technological development.

Religion may seem a strange place to look for technological support. Most major faiths seem either indifferent or outrightly hostile to the technological undertaking — one reason why Vatican II in the 1960s (which praised technology in service of humans) was so refreshing. The Protestant Reformation and its work ethic certainly was conducive to technological growth, yet the Reformation took place after the communication (print) and scientific revolutions had already started. Could there have a been a subtle element in earlier Western religion that perhaps quite unintentionally provided a foundation for the explosion of technology in Europe?

Thinking about this question a few years ago — and having seen a rerun of *The Robe* on some late night TV — I suddenly became struck by a very peculiar and unique element of Roman Catholicism: its miracle of miracles, the return of Christ after his death, was an essentially physical, not purely spiritual, miracle. Of course, most religions have some sort of physical evidence for the Divine occurring from time to time, but only Roman Catholicism has God producing a son born of a human woman, walking and living among humans on Earth, killed, and returning not only in spirit but in flesh. (Greek and earlier pagan religions had many human-god interactions — but these were dispersed among numerous gods, and lacked the intensity of the monotheistic creeds.)

Elaine Pagels' excellent *The Gnostic Gospels* (Random House, 1979) underscores just how crucial the physical return of Christ is in the Roman Catholic dogma. Apparently early Christian sects which did not follow Peter's See insisted that Christ returned only in spirit — in a vision to the Disciples — and not in bodily form. Yet the founders of the Roman Church went out of their way to describe the Resurrection as physical: touch me, I'm real, Christ repeatedly says to the shocked Disciples. Pagels suggests that the builders of the Church shrewdly recognized that this physical return of Christ gave them a unique position of authority in the Christian schema: a spiritual vision can in principle be experienced and claimed by anyone (Christ came to me in my dreams), but a physical return requires physical corroboration, and this was only available via the self-reinforcing testimony of the witnessing Disciples.

Whatever the origins, whether in cosmic truth or religious politics, I'd suggest that the emphasis on Christ's physical transcendence of death gave the Western world an affinity for physical transformations — the stock and soul of technology — lacking or outrightly opposed by other religions.

Historians have long known that most of the great inventions of the world originated in China. Yet there, the spiritual/physical dichotomy — the ultimate purely spiritual success over the worldly in Buddhism, for example — yielded a culture that saw technology as essentially peripheral to the deepest aspects of human existence. (Confucianism, the other great religious system of the East, denigrated the worldly in another way — teaching that the making of personal profit from inventions was immoral. See McNeill's *The Pursuit of Power*, University of Chicago, 1982, for more.)

In the Christian West, 1500 years of Christ's fleshly triumph had created a climate in which the spiritual and the physical were intimately infused, in which spirit triumphed not *over* matter but *with* and *in* and *through* matter. Could this be the real backbone of the modern common sense faith that we humans can reach for the cosmos through the physical transformation of our world and beyond via technology? Could the Christian taste for miracles of physical transcendence have quietly directed the use of technologies for greater and greater alterations of reality, in contrast to the Chinese use of its major inventions of printing and gunpowder primarily on ceremonial occasions?

Intriguing to think that the Roman Catholic Church, which for so much of its history had been a conscious enemy of technological development, was from the very beginning the carrier of an attitude towards spirit and matter which is technology's greatest friend.

IT WHO LAUGHS LAST

I remain fascinated by the differences — and apparent similarities — between machine "thought" and operations, and the human kind.

Several weeks ago, I had occasion to give a talk to a group of visiting Japanese businessmen and educators in New York City. In my usual way, I threw in a goodly number of lame jokes, and was gratified to see the audience laugh quite heartily when the jokes were translated by the able interpreter. Virtually no one in the group spoke more than a word of English.

A few days later I had occasion to chat on the phone with a friend in Tokyo. I told him about my talk, and how fascinated I was to see that, despite all the sociological talk about the relativity of humor, my little sallies had gone over quite well in Japanese translation.

"I wouldn't jump to any conclusions, if I were you," my friend advised, a chuckle in his voice.

"Why not?" I asked.

He proceeded to tell me about a talk given by an Oxford professor in Japan that he had attended a little while ago. This Englishman, like me, was given to tossing in a joke or two with a serious talk. He would deliver his one-liner, then look to the audience in expectation of a laugh. And like me, he wasn't disappointed.

"So why shouldn't I jump to conclusions about the universality of humor — at least mine and this guy's in Tokyo?" I asked my friend.

"Because each time the Oxford prof made a joke," my friend told me, "the translator told the audience (in Japanese):

'Our speaker has just made a little joke. You might consider laughing a bit if you can.'"

Reeling from this revelation, I sought to find some value in it, and discovered a striking relevance to artificial intelligence: Machines think and respond because they are programmed to do so — told to respond just like the polite Japanese audiences. On the behavioral level, this may not matter. Surely the gentleman in Japan enjoyed the Japanese response to his jokes, just as I had in New York.

And yet the thought that my audience in New York laughed because they were advised to, and not because they found my wit of genuine humor, does not thrill me (deep down in my vanity, I'm still sure my guests did indeed get my jokes from the translation). In other words, though two sets of behavior may on the surface be indistinguishable, the programmed nature of one versus the spontaneous nature of the other makes all the difference — at least to me, and satisfaction of my sense of humor, and I suspect to most of us. Painting by the numbers isn't art.

Herein, then, lies the challenge to AI, or at least to those champions of AI who'd like to see it every bit the equivalent of human intelligence: construct a machine, a program, whose performance is not the result of programming — whose behavior can be what existentialists refer to as "authentic" or self-generated.

A cynic might well respond that we humans are ourselves the products of prior conditioning and programming — that laughing at jokes because we find them funny is no less a consequence of previous conditioning than laughter in response to a plea to do so.

Perhaps in the broadest possible sense this is so. Our present attitudes and behavior are indeed products of our past. Yet to call this past, infinitely complex molding of our present a type of "programming" seems to strain the meaning of this word beyond any usefulness.

And so for me, the difference between laughing because you cannot help yourself — because something just tickles your fancy — and laughing because you're advised or expected to, remains enduring. Until AI enthusiasts can bridge this gap, even their greatest creations will just be so much laughing in the dark.

A FIRE NOT WORTH IT

The first four months of 1986 have been unrelievedly grim ones for our species. Of the three shocking events that have thus far occurred — the Challenger explosion, the increase of terrorism and the U.S. raid on Libya, and the nuclear accident near Kiev in the Soviet Union — I think the last by far poses the most serious questions and dangers for human life.

Indeed, although I am (as most of you know) a generally truculent and unapologetic champion of the human technological enterprise (I regard the defeat of the supersonic transport plane or "SST" a decade ago as one of the darkest technological episodes in US history), I have since the trauma of Three Mile Island come to see the use of nuclear (fission) energy for peaceful resource purposes to be an irreconcilable exception.

The grave danger arises precisely because the context for fission energy use is peaceful: I expect that heads of states with nuclear arsenals are more or less sane, and highly unlikely to deliberately initiate a nuclear exchange. Further, the extraordinary nature of the use of nuclear arms works to keep the possibility of accidental nuclear launch or bombing very low. So far, at least, the evidence supports this conclusion.

But not so when fission is used in a workaday generation of energy for peaceful purposes. Here, apparently, the lulling effect of repeated successful operations sets in, and the results are the 15 reported (and likely more) nuclear accidents in civilian operations in the past 30 years.

But accidents happen in all technological endeavors. So what's so different about the ill-consequences of an occasional nuclear energy accident?

The consequences differ by huge magnitudes in terms of the choice people have in being exposed to the risk, the numbers of people exposed, and the duration of the consequences.

On the options people have:

In the case of the Challenger explosion, the deaths — awful though they were both for the victims and humanity as a whole

— were in fact limited to the seven who volunteered for the mission. Plane crashes with few exceptions jeopardize mainly the lives of the passengers, who are (with the exception of children) on the plane as a matter of choice. Even the automobile, criticized as degrading the life quality of Americans who must breathe exhaust fumes, etc., for the most part risks the lives of those who elect to drive or be driven.

Not so the nuclear accident, which in most cases jeopardizes people who never made a decision to build and operate or even utilize a nuclear plant. (The US is less extreme in this regard than the Soviet Union, for we can in theory elect lawmakers who vote to ban plants, etc. The relationship between a political election and the building of a plant is attenuated, however, to the point where this sort of control is rarely exercised.)

About the only other energy form which comes to mind in history as jeopardizing multitudes of unconsenting people is fire itself, which in the 19th century age of kerosene lamps ravaged many an innocent family and even town population.

But whereas the out-of-control fire is limited both in the numbers it can affect (usually not more than a given city at worst — as in the great fire in Chicago last century), and the time the damage lasts (basically ending when the fire itself ends), the parameters of nuclear damage are obviously far greater.

We're talking here about majorities of the world's population (not just one city or area) being radiated to a greater or lesser degree depending upon the amounts of emission, and contaminations of areas very close to the accident lasting for centuries.

No number of inevitably fallible safety procedures can make us secure that events even worse than are now unfolding in Chernobyl won't happen again. Sooner or later, if we continue proliferation of fission plants (or even operation of existing ones), an accident will happen — just as sooner or later, another spacecraft will seriously malfunction. Accident is the way of technology. It's the way we learn.

When the cost is a finite number of human lives, the cost is baneful, but the alternative of scotching the technology may be worse for our species in the long run. The risk of space crews seems worth our migration to the stars.

When the cost can be most of the human population — and populations yet unborn — then the risk of continuing the technology becomes too great, and the risk of stopping the technology acceptable. The risk of much of our planet and our offspring cannot be worth a lower heating bill.

I'd like to see the expeditious phasing out and shut down of all fission power plants on the face of the Earth.

WINGS FOR THE BOUND

Amidst all the important discussion of the uses of online communication to mitigate global disputes and in general help humans on a species-wide level, I thought I'd share with you an account of how online education has made a difference in at least one individual's life (actually two, including mine).

For the past month and a half, Connect Ed has benefited from the participation of a student totally deaf since birth. Remarkable for many years, this person always wanted to make an impact in the world at large — sign language was mastered early on, but the student decided to pursue the same higher education as that available to those without hearing impairment.

The actual process was not easy. The student taped lectures attended in person, and had them transcribed for later reading. Although most of the content was preserved, such an approach engendered a very passive, non-interactive mode of learning.

When I first met this person (I'm deliberately avoiding use of pronouns here so as to in no way compromise this person's identity), I was instantly struck by a vivid twinkle and thirst for knowledge in the eyes. Fortunately, prior experience on Compuserve had given this student rudimentary knowledge of online communication which could be translated rather easily to our online campus.

The intellectual contributions — though fine — have really been the least significant aspect of our relationship, at least for me. Far more gratifying have been the ways we have communicated, the ways our exchanges via this medium have given me a friendship with someone I likely never would have been friends with otherwise. I've learned that a world minus all sound engenders a certain gentleness, at least in my friend, and exposure to this gentle though vibrant mind has proven a real education for me, in the most profound way.

The consideration of technologies — especially computers —often takes the form of lofty, abstract analyses of what this and that device can do for humanity. I'm part of this tendency myself, and think that such analyses are necessary and crucial.

But technologies clearly have different impacts on different people, and what is a luxury or even a real benefit for some may be a basic necessity for others.

For me, and I assume most of you, word processing and computer conferencing have proved marvelous ways to increase the dissemination of our ideas and the stimulation of our minds. These benefits now seem almost essential to me, though I know that my intellect lived pretty well before then.

For my friend, the capacity to commit thoughts to screen where they can immediately or later be responded to is something quite else. For the first time in this person's life, communication can take place with the vast world without any real or social or psychological effect of disability.

Online conferencing has given this person wings that all of us take for granted, and this ultimately may be one of the most important consequences of our medium. It certainly is among the most beautiful.

ICONS AND GARBAGE CANS

Icons are a special form of graphics capability which allow you to command computers by moving a cursor to a cartoon or stick figure type of picture in the corner of the screen, and pressing Enter. Thus, if you want to delete a file, you move your cursor to a cartoon of a garbage can, and press the Enter or Return key. This is supposed to be an improvement over typing "Delete" or "Erase" at a command prompt.

How so? Well, I guess it's easier to misspell (certainly easier to misspell misspell, that's for sure) a word than it is to move a cursor to a picture. On the other hand, most icon programs require you to move the cursor exactly over the icon, or at least fully in the command zone — anything less and the command won't execute, so I guess this constitutes a capacity for misspelling of sorts. Still, I'm willing to grant elimination of errors due to spelling as one advantage of an icon system.

What else? Well, pictures are not usually prone to translation problems. Presumably a garbage can icon would be equally comprehensible to anyone in an old-fashioned paper-laden office in any part of the world — though the offices with new-fangled computer systems that don't use and dispose of so much paper might find the garbage can a bit archaic. And a poor soul in an utterly unindustrialized part of the world would probably be totally out of luck vis-à-vis garbage cans. Still, I'm willing to grant an edge to icons in this category of universal understandability.

What, then, are the deficits in an icon system? I can think of but one: the failure to utilize a system of communication of virtually infinite flexibility and subtlety — one which has been under development by humans for hundreds of thousands of years at least.

I'm thinking here of spoken and written language, misspellings and all. What our species has been about, to a large extent, has been development of a system which allows representation of any thought, concept, image, or object in the universe with a

A CHRONICLE OF AIDS

A danger in this or any new medium is that we talk only amongst ourselves — that we become a self-reinforcing island that has little impact on the rest of the world. To avoid this syndrome I favor "multi-mediation," or sharing of the products of online communication through other older, better established media, such as broadcasting and the printed press.*

And this is one reason that I view as an important event the recent publication of a remarkable book written by Mike Greenly — *Chronicle: The Human Side of AIDS*.** A vivid and sensitive series of interviews with prostitutes, heterosexual drug addicts, gays, a bisexual husband, doctors, nurses, public health officials, and others caught up in the escalating AIDS tragedy, this volume was written entirely online in a series of computer conference comments by Greenly on Parti on the Source.

Greenly is a stunningly effective writer on any topic, and would be in any medium. He's the epitome of the transparent journalist — to read him is to look directly into the faces and souls of the people he interviews — and he asks questions of his subjects that cut to the core of issues with laser-like grace and precision. (I had the pleasure of being interviewed by him several years ago in connection with my Electure on "Space" on The Source. I told him in a typical spurt of egotism after reading the story he did on me that I'd seriously consider his writing my biography some day. I meant it too — though at this point in our careers, Greenly's more likely to have a biography written about him than am I.)

I'm sorry that his book was published by such a small press. Greenly wanted a publication no later than a year after he had started the project — understandable in view of its topicality — and anyone who has ever gone through the interminable rigma-role of getting a book published can sympathize with any move that shortens or lessens the uniquely sapping experience of this exercise.*** (About the only experience equivalently dispiriting is attending a faculty meeting. Actually, faculty meetings are a bit better, but they happen more often and so their cumulative limited series of arbitrary symbols (in the case of the alphabet some 26+). Granted, we have spelling and translation problems — but we also have the capacity, with written (and spoken) language-oriented computer systems, to pair the speed of electricity with the scope of imagination and its ability to convey meaning through words.

True, current text computers can only respond to a limited number of words, and thus in practice are no more flexible than programs that respond only to a limited number of drawings. But which system do you think in the future will be able to respond to more commands: word-based systems which derive their power from the human generative mind, or picture-based systems which derive their power from mimicry of the visual environment? (See my chronicle "Don't Distract Me with the Fax" for more on the differences between analogic-mimicry and digital modes of communication.)

Word processing and its relatives in digital music and image generation have set the mind free from requirements of physical dexterity in creation and communication of thoughts and art. With the bit-represented word or tone or brushstroke, the mind can attain a flexibility and sweep in the outside world that it formally hummed only or mainly to itself. Icons reduce this flexibility to kindergarten dimensions.

effect may be worse.) Still, the book deserves to be published by Random House or Doubleday — who knows, perhaps this small publication will bring the book to the attention of the biggies.

Another pitfall the participants in new media need to take care to avoid is hypostatizing themselves as the first in areas in which they are not. Mike often refers to himself as "the world's first interactive journalist" — this is not true, as there was reporting of events and interviews here on the Electronic Information Exchange System when Parti was less than a gleam in its creators' eyes.

But if Mike Greenly is not the world's first interactive journalist, he is as far as I can tell the best. His book is occasion for celebration not because of its topic, which constitutes one of the grim reapers of our time, but because its publication in paper will give the large offline world a window on a vibrant writer that some of us in the online world have long enjoyed and learned from. Do yourself a favor and read it.

---

*January, 1992: Hence this very book that you are now reading....

**January, 1992: *Chronicle: The Human Side of AIDS* by Mike Greenly (New York: Irvington Publishers, 1986). The book unfortunately has been out of print for several years.

***January, 1992: My reasons for publishing *Electronic Chronicles* with a small press are much the same as Greenly's: time-pertinent text (albeit not, in all instances, dealing with the life-and-death matters of Greenly's). I also find the experience of working directly with the president of the press very satisfying.

THE ENDLESS SIXTIES

Back in 1972, before I had embarked on a life of academe, I worked with Murray "the K" Kaufman, a disc jockey on WNBC-AM Radio in New York City. Murray was acknowledged as the successor of Alan Freed — the father of rock 'n' roll — with his radio show on WINS and his live concerts on stage at the Brooklyn Paramount Theater in the late '50s and early '60s. He was an early appreciator and confidant of the Beatles, for which he earned the name "The Fifth Beatle." He was also a pioneer in the broadcasting of what he called "attitude" music on WOR-FM in 1965 and 1966 — what would later be called underground and then progressive rock. He returned to New York for one of his periodic comebacks in July, 1972. I wrote a column about Murray's return for *The Village Voice* — he called me a day later, and asked me if I'd like to come to work for him as his musical advisor. Mostly what we did is work out segues of records, seamless transitions of one record to another organized around a certain theme or story, that would sometimes be hours in length.

Anyway, Murray was a cerebral fellow, and we'd often talk into the wee hours of the morning about the history and future of popular music. Murray had a theory about revolutions in music coming every nine years — it started in 1927 with the Paul Whiteman Orchestra; then Benny Goodman first hit really big in 1936; Frank Sinatra made them swoon in the aisles of the Paramount in 1945; Presley burst onto the scene in 1954; and the Beatles crossed the Atlantic and became an international sensation as the world reeled from Kennedy's assassination in late 1963. So 1972 was due to be a big year by Murray's theory. The question was when (what month of the year) and who. (Murray had an interest in a new group signed to Epic Records, and secretly hoped it would be them.)

As October rolled into November, and December loomed, our discussions about who would be the Beatles of the '70s grew more urgent. (Murray left WNBC before the end of the year, and so did I.)

They never came. The best that 1972 could offer was Bette Midler and the Bay City Rollers. Interesting, talented, but no revolution in music.

Well, cycles are notoriously undependable. Surely in 1973 some new earth-rocking trend or star would arrive. But 1973 was even more uneventful musically than the year before.

New sorts of music have arisen in the years since then. Disco, punk, new wave all have had their day. And stars like Springsteen and Madonna have made some impact. But nothing to compare with Presley or the Beatles or Sinatra in their days.

I first began toying with an answer in the mid-'70s, and have come to believe it even more strongly in the years since: nothing really new happened in music in 1972 because 1972 was still the '60s, culturally speaking. And we're still in the '60s, more or less, today.

Look at our hair lengths, dress styles, even sexual attitudes — all not only products of the '60s but in many respects literally the same as those of the '60s.* Have we really changed much since then? I have hair over my ears and wear jeans when I teach. I could have done this in the '70s and even the late '60s. But in the early '60s and '50s I likely would've gotten memos from deans for this sort of "casual" attitude towards teaching.

Somehow in the period from the '20s through the '60s, America (and the world) underwent an enormous series of changes vis-à-vis the Victorian culture that held sway throughout the previous century and until World War I. Having grown up in these times, we became accustomed to revolution every decade — Murray's nine year cycle.

But there are other precedents in history — of cultural attitudes that have held for hundreds of years. Wouldn't it be interesting if the '60s were an end not the beginning of a revolutionary cycle, and we and our children will be living in its cultural umbrella until well into the next century?

Chronocentrism on my part? Could be — certainly many of my sensibilities were shaped during that amazing decade.

But I attended my nephew's Bar Mitzvah in Boston last week. And you know what his favorite rock group is today? The Beatles. I understand the same is true in Moscow.

---

*January, 1992: Sexual attitudes in the 1990s may be finally changing under pressure of AIDS. But note how long this has taken, and how resistant 1960s sexual behavior was to earlier, less deadly health concerns, e.g., herpes in the late '70s and early '80s.

SERENDIPITY IN PHOSPHOR
AND HARD COPY

The scene is the Levinson apartment overlooking Van
Cortlandt Park in the northern part of New York City. It's well
past one in the morning, a summer breeze is playing with the
trees, and my family and every sane person in the neighborhood
is sound asleep....

I'm pretty sleepy myself, but I want to take care of one bit
of business before turning in for the night. I'm still putting the
"finishing" touches on *Mind at Large*, and my problem is this:
I've got this great quote by Immanuel Kant, but in my usual
fashion I somehow neglected to make note of the page it's on.

I know the book it's from — Kant's *Critique of Pure Reason*.
And I'm pretty sure I know what part of the book ... but, as I look
and look and browse and read, I become aware of in how many
places Kant says more or less the same thing. None of which are
exactly my quote, though.

It's now past two, and I'm getting bleary-eyed and irritable.
How long do I have to keep looking for one little line? I'm reading
the book page by page now, determined to find this quote, and
the hours are rolling by and still no luck.

If only Kant were in an online database somewhere.
Actually, with optical scanning devices cropping up all over,
Critique of Pure Reason probably *is* available in full form online
somewhere, but at three o'clock in the morning I'm too tired to
think of where this might be. As the time nears four, I begin to
toy with the idea of taking Kant's quote out of my book — it's
tempting, but I just can't bring myself to do it. I finally throw the
book down after four, and go to sleep, disgruntled.

Next morning I'm at it again. My 2½ year old son, seeing
I'm reading, collects a whole bunch of *his* books and dumps them
on my lap. "Here, see if you can find the page where Kant talks
about extending knowledge beyond the bounds of sensory
experience," I say, handing him Kant's book in return.

Later that day, I found the quote. A total of nearly six hours spent, I reckon, in tracking down that one line.

A powerful argument in favor of the electronic library, yes? Had *Pure Reason* been online and accessible by me, I could have located that quote in less than six minutes.

But then again, I wouldn't have been obliged to re-read *The Critique of Pure Reason*, in which process I discovered four additional Kant gems, and deepened my understanding of this book. Last time I read *Pure Reason* so carefully was better than eight years ago, when I knew much less than I know now.

Sometime very soon, *Pure Reason* and the great texts will likely all be accessible to everyone with a personal computer and modem.* And browsing and serendipity will play roles in electronic research that we can only dimly imagine now. And yet I'd wager that folks searching for that elusive quote will not quite have the advantage I and all the other poor beggars after knowledge have had over the past thousands of years when looking through books and manuscripts.

There's still something to be said for the book.

---

*January, 1992: The "Past Masters" series (InteLex Corp., PO Box 1827, Clayton, GA 30525) has an impressive array of philosophy texts now on disk, including Aquinas, Hobbes, Locke, Hume, Bentham, J.S. Mill, Sedgwick, Machiavelli, Rousseau, Burke, Paine, Kierkegaard, Descartes, Leibniz, Spinoza, Adam Smith, and Ricardo. InteLex's representative told me Kant's *Critique of Pure Reason* is now available on disk in English translation from Oxford University Press and Books in Philosophy (two different editions). Getting these electronic texts into an online database accessible via personal computer and modem is an easy job.

THE BUSINESS OF GOVERNMENT
IN SPACE

On a rainy afternoon in Boston several years ago, I found myself sitting next to David Thompson of the Orbital Sciences Corporation over lunch in the Legal Seafoods restaurant. Thompson was in attendance at the Conference on Space Context and Opportunity convened by Apollo astronaut Rusty Schweickart and MIT Professor Kosta Tsipis at MIT. (My paper "Cosmos Helps Those Who Help Themselves: Historical Patterns of Technological Fulfillment, and their Applicability to the Human Development of Space," in *Research in Philosophy & Technology*, ed. C. Mitcham, JAI Press, 1989, provides a description of what I said at that conference.)

Thompson was a young entrepreneur with a gleam in his eye and a fervor in his bearing that spoke of the possibility of someday doing big things. At the time, though, his company was new and struggling, scavenging a contract hither and yon to help build a satellite or contribute to the construction of a launch device.

I asked him what he thought was the main obstacle to his business.

"Government," he answered immediately. Not a question of taxes or red tape or the usual problems business people have with the government, but a simple problem of competition. "We never know when and if NASA may start offering the same services we do, for a cheaper price." The mere possibility of NASA involvement in commercial space enterprises cast a pall over entrepreneurs like Thompson moving into commercial space development.

Thompson's plaint found a ready recipient in a laissez-faire governmental minimalist like me. What legitimate role does government have in society other than safeguarding the lives of its citizens? In industrial and post-industrial (i.e., informational) environments, surely the government ought do its best to create a climate that facilitates growth. But does the government's going into business serve such a climate? In Thompson's case, the answer was no.

A New York banker also in attendance at the Space Conference made a suggestion for government involvement in space commercialization that was welcomed by Thompson. Insurance for space enterprises is almost impossible to come by (and impossibly high when it is) in the aftermath of the Challenger. How about the government insuring would-be space insurers, or providing an insurance of last resort for space projects, much in the way that the Federal Reserve now guarantees deposits (up to a limit) in local banks?

Ronald Reagan, to his credit, decided to de-commercialize NASA (I view Reagan as second only to JFK as an American president who inspired and gave positive leadership to the space program). This enabled David Thompson to breathe easier, but it wasn't and isn't enough — the government ought to provide insurance as indicated above, tax credits and incentives for those who invest in space, do what it can to uncork the power of free enterprise in our movement into space.

Ivan Bekey, then Director of Advanced Planning at NASA, was also at the MIT conference. In a riveting paper, he described some of the projects that Advanced Planning had on the drawing boards for the past two decades. He spoke of solar sail ships to other solar systems, self-replicating electronic mechanisms on the moon and Mars and beyond, probes to the moons of Jupiter and Saturn, the beginnings of human habitation on the asteroids.

Such vision, powered by private not government financing, may ultimately be our best route to the stars. Biosphere II, a privately funded commercial venture in which eight people and countless plants and organisms are to be sealed in a physically closed but informationally open environment — much as would be the case in an interplanetary spacecraft, except that Biosphere II will be rooted on Earth, in Arizona, not space — is a first example of such commercially-engined science. Our challenge in the 21st century will be to create an economic climate that can actually launch and sustain such a vehicle in the highways beyond Earth.

BEATLES ON THE BEACH

Among the many creatures who live along the shore of Cape Cod Bay, we humans are among the most fascinating.

To the chalky browns and yellows of the sand, the vivid greens of the grasses, and the infinity of blue-green shades reflected in the water and the sky, we add the light orange of sailboat and bright red of bikini on a given summer's day.

To the cry of gulls and whoosh of water washing and draining on the shore, we add the chatter of a hundred voices, the laughter and squeals of kids running in the waves.

And something more. Somewhere in the distance, a faint "la la la" and the twang of electric guitars. A transistor tuned into a local radio station is playing the Beatles "You Won't See Me."

So easy to take for granted, but so strange, really, to hear this music now in the sands of Brewster, Massachusetts. First released more than twenty years ago as one of many superb cuts in the *Rubber Soul* album, one of the first successful albums without a leading hit record, and one of the first of a group of new songs to be played on the newly liberated FM Radio. (The FCC in 1966 had asked AM stations owning FM stations to make sure that they broadcast substantially different content — or else relinquish license on one or the other — and this had stimulated the otherwise stagnant FM stations to experiment with new music. A rare case of a positive artistic result arising from a government decree.)

What is so remarkable about hearing "You Won't See Me" on a Cape Cod beach — and what we take for granted — is that the record sounds exactly as it did at the time it was released (and for that matter, at the time its voices and sounds were recorded) decades ago in London. Of course it should — it's the same record. But what else in nature, or even the human world, remains unchanged to a syncopation after 20 years?

Not the sands and contours of the shore, which although maintaining something of a statistical average when erosion doesn't take its toll, nonetheless shift and slide in innumerable ways in a 20 week, let alone a 20 year, period. Not the sounds of birds or even humans, who come and go with the days and seasons, incessantly adding a voice here, subtracting a sound there, from the acoustic shore melange.

Not even the books that humans read, or the carvings which our ancestors made in places around the world as long as millennia ago. For though the letters and words may endure unchanged, they provide even in their birth but a second-hand glimpse into the thoughts and emotions and realities they describe. They were born noisy, and the most careful preservation can at best make sure that this noise — this profound indirectness of the abstract word — does not increase.

Music is different. It speaks to and from something very direct in the human being. Until recently, it endured only via desiccation into notation — a transformation into a recipe, which had to then be actualized anew by each talented or untalented musician who sought to bring this music to life.

Sound recording in its own modest way has changed all that. The sounds of our lives and popular cultures exist for our taking, any time we want, from virtually anyplace in the world. More importantly, they — along with companion recorded arts of film and video and photography — endure in vital, fluid reality, as fresh today as the day they were recorded.

Is this the end of popular culture, in the sense that Heidegger spoke of technology spelling the end of philosophy? Does perfect preservation run counter to the evolutionary impulse from which novelty and originality emerge?

Or is this the end of popular culture in another sense that Heidegger likely also intended: the end as an Aristotelian final cause: a goal.

As I walked down the shore and the water ran from my toes I heard Paul McCartney's fingers squeaking on the strings of a bass guitar two decades ago. The freeze frame of human impulse is upon the universe.

TECHNOLOGICAL BACK-UP:
SUSPENDERS AND A BELT
ARE NOT ENOUGH

A continuing legacy of Challenger and Chernobyl is a renewed concern for technological back-up and safety systems — their necessity, their dependability, making them human-proof, and perhaps most of all, the question of how much redundancy in back-up is advisable.

Clearly we have a law of diminishing returns in back-up redundancy. The third level of back-up provides a greater margin of safety than the hundredth and third.

But let me share with you a true story that happened to me. A story that demonstrates that when it comes to technology, no level of back-up can ever confidently be deemed totally sufficient.

We returned to New York City after six delightful weeks on Cape Cod at the end of last summer. One of the things I'd been working on was completion of my book *Mind at Large.* In particular, I'd been working hard on the footnotes.

These came to about 300 "K," in computer storage lingo, of material (probably more than 100 pages). Since later notes in the book refer to earlier notes, which in turn are always subject to minor emendation, I elected to keep this material entirely on disk — no paper printout. But wait a minute — I'm not as crazy as you think! By keeping this on disk, I mean I had three independent copies of the material: (a) on the hard disk of my main pc, (b) on a floppy disk that could be read by any pc, and (c) on a specially formatted floppy disk that could be read either by any pc or an ancient workhorse of a computer that I keep in a closet in my office (an old CP/M machine).

This seemed like more than enough back-up, but before we began disconnecting and packing up equipment, I asked my wife Tina if perhaps I should take the time — at least two hours — to print out all this stuff on paper. I explained to her that I could think of virtually no scenario that would endanger all three of these independent disk sources. She told me, "I still don't want to even think of being on the same planet with you if something should somehow go wrong with all three copies. Do the paper print out." While I was mulling this over, a friend dropped by and asked if we would like to go for a walk on the beach ...

Well, here we are back in New York City — it's Labor Day morning, and family and equipment and data are safe and sound. I turn on my main pc and ... nothing. No action — the screen just stupidly flickers without engaging the hard disk. After trying to revive the machine for better than an hour, I realize that this heap of silicon and whatever needs a dealer's attention. This could always endanger the data.

Oh well... I've got my ancient office machine and my back up pc at home. I take the back up out, set it up, plug in the wires and ... discover that the cord that connects the keyboard to the back of the machine doesn't seem to fit right. Upon examination, I see that my 2¾ year old son had somehow stuck a pencil into the receiving slot for the brief minute or two the machine was out in the open last year.

Just then the phone rang: the faculty are striking at my school, the caller tells me, and I won't have access to my office!

Meanwhile, my publisher expected a manuscript in the mail last week....

The moral of the story: when it comes to technology, even suspenders and a belt are not enough: you'd better glue the pants to your skin.

Oh yes: I did take Tina's advice and made the paper copy after all. Also, I've now restored my personal computers to full service, and I'm typing this chronicle on it right now.

But this whole episode was too, too close a call for my liking. From now on, I'm going to do paper printouts at least every 10K.

Sure I will. And if I click my heals together three times I'll be somewhere in Kansas.

COMPUTER CONFERENCING
AND THE PERSONALIZATION
OF SCHOLARLY PUBLISHING

The uneasy relationship of social custom and technological innovation has often been remarked upon by observers of society and technology. The problem is that the two are rarely in harmony: new technologies undermine cherished social values, and deeply ingrained customs stifle the development and implementation of inventions. The social custom and technological underpinning of scholarly publishing has been as much a victim as a reporter of these problems, and is indeed in need of fine tuning right now to adjust itself to new electronic media.

Until at least the end of the 19th century, scholarly publishing was characterized by two important procedures: (a) individual editors read manuscripts submitted to book or journal publishers, and made decisions on whether the material should be printed, (b) all modes of logic and evidence were considered acceptable support for a theory or idea — this included anecdotal, introspective analyses, as well as what we now would call data from experiments and statistics.

Massive improvements in the efficiency of publication in the 19th century greatly increased the numbers of possible publications, and the supply rose to meet the wide contours of this new channel. As the 20th century progressed, publishers were deluged with manuscripts and proposals — further, such plums as academic tenure became dependent on literal number of publications. For these and related reasons, editors and publishers became increasingly "objective" in their criteria for publication. Editors no longer made publishing decisions on their own — they submitted texts to "outside" readers, who give texts a presumably blind review. (The results of these readings often suggest that the readers are indeed blind. But the term refers to the author's identity kept anonymous in these evaluations. Indeed, authors and readers have little if any opportunity for dialogue — the author receives the readers' views much like a person on trial in a star chamber proceeding.) Further, the notion of acceptable support for an argument changed from the somewhat subjective criterion of judging an author's logic to a demand for objective statistical verification of arguments.

Most observers agree that the system is flawed. The Cyril Burt affair in England a few years ago (wherein a famous researcher was found to have totally forged statistics), admissions by readers that they in fact were able to guess the author's identity, and like problems have shown that the ideal of objective publishing is difficult to maintain. But till now no other alternatives seemed workable.

I suggest that the availability of computer conferencing and electronic text transfer may offer a solution to the problem. While the notion of anonymous dialogue through paper mail is somewhat absurd, such exchanges could occur and occur quite effectively in an online environment. In such an electronic text situation, authors would be free to question and probe the readers for clarification of comments. Publishers could review an entire exchange between author and reviewer and make a decision on that basis, rather than merely on the basis of an outside review and perhaps one out-of-context paper response from the author (as is now the case.)

Moreover, the re-emphasis of dialogue might have a beneficial effect on the problem of statistics being seen as the only reliable mode of evidence in many fields. The easy availability of written discussion via computer conferencing may make such discussion more accessible as a means of scholarly support.

These and other possibilities are being considered by several groups of which I'm a member. We can expect electronically refereed journals to begin appearing as soon as the end of this year. I'll keep you posted.*

---

*January, 1992: In January 1990, I was appointed Editor-in-Chief of the *Journal of Social and Biological Structures*. Among my first acts was reduction of number of articles chosen for publication by blind external review, and reliance instead on editorial selection — mine — for acceptance/rejection of articles for publication. In the past two years, some 80 percent of our articles have been selected in this fashion, and we are very pleased with the results. My basic credo in editing is that if the editor cannot on his or her own have time and understanding sufficient to make a publication decision about an article pertinent to the journal's interests, the editor has no business editing the journal. Further, associate editors, not blind outside reviewers, should be the editor's next resource in publication decisions. *JSBS* already has some of its editorial staff online, and we expect to do more of our work online in the coming years. The *Journal* is published by JAI Press in Greenwich, Connecticut, and a hypertext version is available on disk or via modem from Connected Education.

"DALLAS" GETS METAPHYSICAL AND LOSES ITS CENTS OF REALITY

An ancient and still extant mystic question asks: how do you know that your dreams are not reality and what you wake up to each morning not your dream? These questions unnerve all but the most truthful philosophers — who are willing to admit that our belief in reality is ultimately a question of faith and belief, logically unprovable — and the solipsist's insistence that the world is his or her dream, equally incapable of dislodgement by logic.

This past Friday the CBS-TV program *Dallas* made its contribution to this old conundrum, feeding millions of Americans a story line that made a whole TV season one character's dream! Unprecedented in the annals of philosophy and television alike....

For those of you who may have spent the past year in a Biosphere closed even to TV information, the background is briefly as follows: The actor who plays Bobby Ewing (characters are always more real than actors) wanted to leave the *Dallas* show. Further, he was sure he was never going to return, so he wanted to be written out in a clear, unambiguous way. No going down in a plane which isn't found or being lost in a forest. So they hit poor Bobby head-on with a car. In the last scene of the season (this was two years ago), Bobby's life monitor flattens and the family stands around the departed in tears. A nice touch to all of this was that Pam, Bobby's divorced wife, had finally gotten back together with Bobby the night before his death. Indeed, they were to be married again.

The next season was not too good ratings-wise* — it seemed as if viewers missed Bobby. Actually, my personal view was that the show was a lot better without this wimp. His absence certainly allowed for interesting character development of most of the other players, including the notorious JR, who actually began to seem human in his brother's absence. But the almighty ratings, as I say, were not so high, and so when Bobby's actor expressed an interest in returning ... the producers of the show had no commercial choice but to comply...

[Here let me just interject that, however much Dickens and Rubens may have been commercially motivated in their own ways, these practitioners and genres do not hold a candle to the commercial determinism of today's TV. When watching this medium, one can literally see plot lines moved hither and thither in slow motion pursuit of a few extra viewers.... But to continue....]

There traditionally are a number of fairly respectable (if implausible) ways of bringing people back from the dead on TV. The most common is that the person didn't really die — cops spirited the severely wounded person out of the limelight, and left a dummy in the bed to fool the fiends who were still out to kill said wounded person. Such a move stretches credibility a bit, I admit, but at least it does no injury to our metaphysics.

Another gambit, not all that common really in soap operas, but cropping up more than ever in science fiction, is the "evil twin." This has a certain amount of sex appeal — here you think you're going to bed with the person you've become nice and cuddly with over the years, when in fact it's a wicked vamp or devil with the same body. Again, stretching it a bit, but not ipso facto impossible and a bit appealing in its way.

[Second interjection: You know what really bothers me? I *liked* last year's plot developments on *Dallas*. The dummy in bed or the evil twin — either one — would have preserved last year's developments in this season's return of Bobby. But the producers had to do something different...]

You likely already know what they did: they made the whole last season Pamela Ewing's dream! A whole season wiped out, just like that Bobby was never hit by the car. He never died in that hospital, his last words croaking out "Be a family..." JR never became a mentsch, Sue Ellen didn't finally overcome her drinking problem, and....

I'm annoyed. I don't know what to believe anymore. It's like I put this comment in Electronic Chronicles online here in good faith, and some computer hacker or programmer snuck in in the middle of the night and changed it!

I guess my mistake is that, like Coleridge's perceiver of the poetic experience, I suspended my disbelief and took television a hair too seriously.

I'll never believe that television is real again.

---

*January, 1992: The success of *Dallas* minus Bobby Ewing that I mentioned in "When One VCR Just Isn't Enough" was alas shortlived.

PRINT AS HAZARDOUS PROPHECY

As the tension between print and electronic means of communication continues, the following revelation has come to light: the January 1986 issue of the Colorado Education Association's journal carried a front page report that all went well with Christa McAuliffe's space shuttle flight. Photographs and several pages of print informed readers that millions of children listened as she gave lessons from space orbit.

This is not the first time that the pressures of print publication have fixed in black and white an utter fantasy — the 1948 newspaper heralding the election to the presidency of Thomas Dewey comes to mind. And yet our educators and our popular judgement continue to hold print as the best record of truth, when in fact quite the opposite may be the case.

Reverence for the written word is comparatively new, historically speaking. Socrates decries writing as a "misbegotten image of the spoken original" (*Phaedrus*), and as late as the Middle Ages, preferred testimony and evidence of contractual relations was verbal, not written. The word "verdict" still embodies the close connection between truth ("ver") and speech ("dict") — a truth spoken, or a finding truly spoken, not written.

By the end of the 19th century, though, the aura of the oral had faded somewhat, as the last syllable of telephone became the word for cheaply artificial (phoney). Print had become the standard of excellence.

The logic behind print's clout is precisely that it is immutable, and thus presumably unmanipulable after publication. When print confines itself to reporting about what has already happened, this immutability is indeed a benefit. But when print dares to report what is essentially prophecy as fact, then quite the reverse obtains. In our fast paced world, much of what we regard as news is a continuum from recent past to this instant to the near future. Attempts to fit this continuum into the Procrustean bed of fixed letters runs the risk of the absurd and the macabre.

But the pull of print remains strong. Our very language, our metaphors of truth and conduct, are now laced with the structures of letters on a page. We want to see it "in black and white." We're advised to get our "thoughts down on paper." The height of conformity is "living by the letter."

But are letters the exclusive feature of print and paper? No — they flourish on computer screens, in smooth defiance of the old view that print and electronics are somehow locked in a battle for the soul of our culture, with the literacy of print under attack from the sensory stimulation and illusion of electronic media. Even before the age of computers, this was not so. The invention of the electric light did more to support the habit of reading than any other invention in history save the printing press itself.

And computers, whatever their screens may resemble, are not television sets: the former provide an alternate medium for literacy, whereas the latter indeed distract (beneficially so, on occasion) from reading. To urge that newspapers and publications of a topical nature be made readily available in electronic format is to urge an improvement, not a reduction, of literary practice.

Paper has and will continue to have its uses and moments. Texts no longer in a position to be changed by their authors need not be transformed into high and low voltages (the basis of the computer's on/off sequences) too quickly. Bound books by great authors of the past will endure with their patinas of wisdom.

But newspapers and newsletters — always fit to wrap tomorrow's fish in in any case — are a different story. Here we would do better to read these modes of reporting online, where the flexibility of electronic letters provides a closer match to the pulsing unpredictability of reality.

(Other chronicles on related themes: "Seeing Edward R. Murrow Now" for television; "A Chronicle of AIDS" for online reporting.)

SDI: THE HISTORY OF TECHNOLOGY AND THE FUTURE OF OUR SPECIES

In the aftermath of the Gorbachev-Reagan Iceland summit — and the failure to reach an agreement due to the US insistence on not abandoning the Strategic Defense Initiative — an understanding of SDI in the context of the history and philosophy of science and technology becomes more important than ever.

Briefly, the goal of SDI is to render nuclear weapons "impotent and obsolete" (this from President Reagan's oft-quoted major speech on the subject). The US opponents of SDI would welcome a defusing of nuclear weapons, but not via an SDI development which they see as counterproductive. In particular, opponents of SDI say it is (a) scientifically impossible and (b) likely to unhinge the precarious balance of terror between the US and the Soviet Union by which we've thus far managed to survive.

The Soviet insistence in Iceland that we abandon SDI should at very least give pause for thought to the holders of the above two arguments against SDI: for although the failure to reach an accord may be evidence of a Soviet perception of "b" (i.e., the Soviets are afraid that a US deployment of SDI would make the US more powerful than the Soviets in reality and in international image), the Soviet response is also a weighty argument against "a". Clearly, Soviet scientists must be telling their leaders that although the Soviet Union has no likelihood of developing an SDI program, the US scientific community does. If not, then why would the Soviets be willing to hold the greatest arms accord in history hostage to SDI? Would they behave in such a way if they really believed that SDI were a pipe dream?

I have written long and often about the hazards of judging any technological accomplishment impossible by current scientific standards. The history of technology is by and large a history of implementing what was previously judged impossible by the world's leading experts.

Here's yet another example: Heinrich Hertz, discover of the electromagnetic waves theoretically predicted by Maxwell, flatly predicted that their use for any widespread means of telecommunication was impossible. It would take a receiving apparatus as big as a whole nation, he quipped, to use his electromagnetic waves as carriers of information.

Marconi, who ignored Hertz's advice and invented radio, said the following about his invention years later: "Long experience has ... taught me not to believe in the limitations indicated by purely theoretical considerations. These — as we well know — are based on insufficient knowledge of all the relevant factors" (cited in W. Edmondson, ed. *The Age of Access: The Posthumous Papers of Colin Cherry* [Dover, NH: Croom Helm, 1985], p. 23).

So added to the seriousness with which the Soviets take SDI, we have the testimony of history.

But why do we need SDI? Assuming that the Soviets are sincere about reducing and perhaps even eliminating nuclear weapons (an assumption which I think we must risk making), I see two crucial reasons in favor of SDI, again taken from history and technology studies:

1. Technologies and information about them are inherently leaky. In the 21st century, we can expect numerous nations to have missiles with warhead capabilities. What protection will we — and the Soviets, for that matter — have against them?

2. Assassinations have altered the course of events numerous times in history, including our own century. What would happen to the Soviet promise to reduce and eliminate nuclear weapons were Gorbachev to be assassinated next year?

The elimination of nuclear weapons is the most important immediate task facing our species. I was born in 1947, had no say in the construction and development of those monstrous weapons, and would do anything I could to see them banished to the dust bins of history before they banish us.

Which is why I support the reduction of nuclear weapons via treaty *and* attempts to render them ineffective via technology.

The two together — treaties and defensive technologies — offer the best assurance that we might survive this insanity we've gotten ourselves into.

Reagan made the right decision at Reykjavik.

PHOSPHOR MAKES INROADS
ON THE ACADEMIC FRONT

Two interesting developments on the electronic front:

• The Fall 1986 MLA (Modern Language Association) Newsletter reported the results of a survey conducted among its members on the question of whether refereed material published in non-print forms (microforms, electronic text journals, etc.) should be given the same weight as print publications in decisions on academic tenure and promotion: 41% favored an equal status for print and electronic publication; but nearly as many respondents didn't care one way or the other, and, significantly, some 21% were actively opposed to equal footing for print and electronic publication (they see print as superior).

• The new edition of the influential *Chicago Manual of Style* is to have a special supplement instructing authors and publishers on how to make the most out of electronically composed (word processed) and communicated (telecommunicated) manuscripts.

So the battle to give electronic publication equal rights in the academic community continues, with phosphor slowly but surely gaining ground.

The tendency to view new modes of communication as aesthetically and even morally inferior to established forms runs deep in our history, as I've mentioned here several times before. Elizabeth Eisenstein reports in *The Printing Press as an Agent of Change* (Cambridge Univ. Press, 1979) that monks were advised for years after the invention of the printing press to continue copying manuscripts by hand — idle hands make the Devil's tools, or some similar view, was apparently the reasoning here.

Shortly after the turn of our own century, D. W. Griffith revolutionized film-making in virtually every way, by moving the camera up, down, sideways, all over the place and away from the proscenium arch which had been dictated by the spirit of live theater. And yet Griffith considered himself unfulfilled because he did not do his great work in the "legitimate" theater. Indeed, the "flick" was for many years considered a cheap substitute for theater, and has moved up the aesthetic ladder only due to the grace of television serving as the new pop cultural whipping boy.

What, other than the emotional investment that so many of us have in paper, could have motivated those 21 % who seriously think that a publication in an electronically communicated journal is ipso facto inferior to publication in a print journal? The numbers of people who read the journal cannot be the issue, for some of our most prestigious scholarly publications are read by people counted in the hundreds. The quality of paper as opposed to phosphor should not be germane, because the actual paper used in many scholarly journals is notoriously poor and subject to yellowing.

Indeed, the electronically published article seems superior in both its viability and its ultimate accessibility: for once published electronically (committed to an online data base of some sort), an article is in principle readable by anyone in the world with a personal computer (or dumb terminal) and a modem. At last count, these numbered easily in the multi-millions.

Published books are another matter, for they are part of an extensively developed series of distributional networks which can churn out millions of copies in relatively short periods of time. I still consider the bound paper book to be the most impressive of publications.

But print publications of scholarly articles are not distributed by such networks.

At my next faculty meeting, I intend to introduce a motion about awarding of tenure and consideration for promotion: the motion will be that from now on electronic publication of scholarly articles be rated *above* print publication in faculty status decisions.

(I'd probably have to form my own electronic faculty for such a motion to pass.... Well, that's one advantage of Connected Education.)

BASEBALL: THE PASTIME OF REASON

Today seems like a good time to write a bit about baseball: neither team has yet won the World Series, so fans of both ballclubs can still feel nothing but good things about the game. These include lifelong Yankee fans like me who have some residual loyalty to our other New York team, and masochists who make a habit of rooting for the Boston Red Sox.

I've been drawn to baseball and its derivatives far more than to any other sport ever since I was a kid. Here in New York the biggest derivatives were stickball and punchball, and the latter was *de rigueur* at least 20 times a week where I grew up in the Bronx.

Watching baseball on TV was also a major spring and summer activity, and, despite the mystique of the physical ballpark, most of the people that I knew learned far more about baseball from Mel Allen's broadcast coverage than from in-person attendance of games.

But by the 1960s, football was attracting a growing television audience, and some were even saying that football was becoming our new national pastime. McLuhan pointed out that the fast flowing simultaneity of football — lots of offensive action happening at once — is much more suited to the electronic age than is the linear, individual hit-the-ball-and-run of baseball.

McLuhan, as usual, was on to something, and I think that much of baseball's appeal comes from its leisurely, linear Victorian style. Indeed, unlike virtually all other major league sports which must end after some number of overtimes — either in a tie or sudden death victory — baseball can go on forever, and cannot end in a tie unless extraordinarily called for by a tired umpire. Whereas football and basketball and "goal" sports cater to the nagging ambiguities and loose ends of the 20th century, baseball upholds the Age of Reason belief in clear-cut objective conclusions.

Baseball differs in other ways. The comedian-philosopher George Carlin points out that while the *modus operandi* of football is to tackle or physically dominate the adversary, in baseball the ball can be dominated (hit, caught, pitched for strikes, etc.) without attacking any person. Football seeks to invade and conquer the other team's goal; baseball wants only to bring its base-runners home. Elevating these observations just a small way, we might say that the philosophy of goal sports is human over human, whereas the philosophy of baseball is more human over nature.

But what I like most about baseball is its recalcitrant individualism, a quality also at its zenith in many ways in the laissez-faire 19th century. More so than any other sport, baseball allows every person on the team the opportunity of becoming a hero. A basket in basketball, a touchdown in football, is difficult to attain without some team support. But when a batter faces the pitcher, the batter at that point has the power with a single well-placed stroke to make an often decisive contribution to the game. (Same with the masterful pitcher who throws a well-paced slider to win the game.)

The life of reason teaches that a single well-placed argument can turn around the beliefs of millions, and make a difference in our social evolution. This is a life that finds its expression in the game of summer and the autumn classic.

INVASIVE MEDIA
OF THE BLOODSTREAM

Continuing concern about drug abuse has led to calls for mandatory drug tests for varieties of groups, including law enforcement officials, athletes (many of whom are already obliged to submit to such tests), and school-age children. The clear implication is that society as a whole would be better were everyone tested for drug usage at regular intervals — perhaps in a manner akin to tests for vision at a driver's license renewal time.

The seesaw between protecting the public health and wellbeing and respecting the privacy of individuals did not begin with the drug abuse problem, but comes into especially sharp focus on this issue. For while the need to combat the death and psychological ruination propagated by drug abuse since the 1960s has been great, the threats to individual liberties in mandatory drug testing is also of a magnitude that far exceeds previous incursions.

Till now the main attempts at combatting drug abuse — in addition to traditional law enforcement techniques — have been directed at what we might call "external" factors, ranging from search and seizure of drugs on individuals, to attempts to regulate the flow of information about drugs in our popular culture. The latter approach reached its height in the early 1970s, when the FCC issued a memorandum to radio stations warning them that their licenses might be in jeopardy if they broadcast songs which glorified drug usage. In fact the main victim of this pressure were songs that condemned drug abuse — e.g., the Temptations' "Cloud Nine" — but which frightened (or the acoustic equivalent of illiterate) radio station programmers decided not to play anyway. (See "Rock 'n' Roll vs. the Arbiters of Decency" in these Chronicles for more on the victimization of rock music by the establishment, and "Naughty Words and Obscene Censorship" for more on the FCC.)

The idea that people have their bodies violated in attempts to uncover drug usage is something pretty new, and something which gives totalitarian shivers, at least to me. For the problem is that once our blood becomes a publicly accessible feature of our existence, all sorts of heretofore highly personal aspects of our lives become open to public scrutiny.

Consider... in addition to uncovering traces of any illegal drugs, mandatory testing of blood could also tell the testers:

- whether the testee was pregnant
- whether the testee was in fact even taking birth control pills
- the whole range of possible legal drugs the testee was taking, thereby revealing to the testers the whole range of illnesses the testee might have (the testing could also directly look for evidence of illnesses of public concern, such as AIDS).

Laws of course could be enacted severely penalizing any drug testing that assessed blood for any non-illegal-drug factors. But the fact still would remain that in making testing of blood for drugs mandatory, we would be giving the government, our employers, and indeed the whole world a technological access to the interiors of our very bodies.

Governments undeniably have the right — indeed the responsibility — to take steps designed to protect the public welfare. Individuals who would use their rights to privacy to subvert the public welfare pose a genuine problem to governments which respect individual privacy but are bound to protect the public. Certainly no one should allow the privacy of a person who, say, harbored a dangerously infectious disease to prevent health officials from identifying this person and taking steps to see that the disease does not spread. Similarly, a reasonable case might be made for mandatory HIV testing among health professionals like dentists, who regularly cut into patients' mouths. (And certainly, mandatory testing of prostitutes makes sense.)

But drug abuse is, as virtually everyone agrees, a fundamentally social not biological problem. To employ technologies on an unrefusable basis that compromise the biological distinction between the inside and the outside of our skin — the physical essence of what makes you and me individual people in distinction to each other and the world we live in — is to risk compromising our humanity in a way that may exceed even the ravages of the drug abuse and the illness this is designed to curtail.

ASIMOV ON GAIA

A little more than a year has passed since I wrote a chronicle entitled "Philosophy in SF Clothing," inspired by reading Isaac Asimov's *Robots and Empire*, the fifth novel in his robot series stretching back to the 1950s.

In that chronicle, I pointed out that science fiction — still regarded as in some sense a second rate form of literature by the literary establishment (you'll rarely find a review of a science fiction novel in the *New York Times Book Review* outside of its special, abbreviated science fiction column) — became in the hands of Asimov, Frank Herbert, and others one of the most lucid conveyors of science and philosophy in our time.

Asimov's latest novel — *Foundation and Earth* (the fifth novel in Asimov's equally old *Foundation* series, which has been ingeniously stitched together with the once independent robot series, now making a continuing series of more than 10 volumes) — irks me more strongly than ever about the loss to our society of not taking science fiction seriously. The book is among the best science books I've read in the past year, and easily among the best in currently written philosophy.

The search for Earth by representatives of distant future human civilizations that have forgotten (or perhaps been deliberately deprived of) precise knowledge of their Earthly origins sets the stage for such scientific-philosophic considerations as:

• an intimate look at the workings of a Gaia planet-society that is more than the metaphor that Gaia is to current Earth;

• speculations on why dolphins haven't developed a technological intelligence: the necessity of fire to the development of technology, and the incompatibility of fire and water;

• the possible role of the moon's gravitation in development of genetic variations (and thus evolution) on Earth;

• scenarios of what happens to a humanly re-arranged ("terraformed") planet if and when humans leave or vanish (in one case, the world goes literally to the dogs.)

But as in all of Asimov's *Foundation* stories, the central question treated from a variety of perspectives is: can the human future be predicted/determined, or are our futures inextricably a product of our individual and unpredictable free wills?

The free-will/determinism question has for quite some time occupied religious thinkers and scientists, both of whom agreed (for different reasons) in the 18th century that the future is fixed from the very beginning. Thus the science of de la Mettrie and LaPlace posited a clockwork mechanism for the universe — total knowledge of which at any one time in principle could provide knowledge of all future time, in much the same way as religions saw (and sometimes still see) all fate sealed in the initial vision of the Deity.

In the 20th century, however, indeterminism has reigned supreme, with the thrust of quantum mechanics suggesting that existence on the most fundamental level may be malleable according to the dictates of individual observation.

My own view — like Karl Popper's — is that both of the above are wrong: the world has objective reality and existence (*contra* some interpretations of quantum mechanics) but is nonetheless in principle unpredictable and non-determinable (for a pre-determined world would make the exercise of rationality and free will a sham, and rationality is the very process which we need to evaluate this question).

Asimov has kept his readers in see-saw suspense on this question for forty years — ending one novel with the impression that futures can be predicted and determined, another with the jolt that the ending of the first was feigned, and more recent novels with suggestions that perhaps determinism was at work all along.... (For those who have read some of Asimov: the predictability/determinism issue revolves around the "Seldon Plan" — a statistical, sort of Club of Rome projection of Galactic futures — and its capacity for predicting and shaping the future with and without a melange of active interventions pro and con the Plan.)

I'm hoping that Asimov will in the ultimate opt for free will. But no matter — I've already found that the reading of his plots since I was 10 in the 1950s has provided some of the most fruitful interludes for thought about these and related issues I've ever encountered.

"MIAMI" SYMBIOSIS

NBC's *Miami Vice* is giving CBS' long standing *Dallas* a run for its money. Beyond the differences in star appeal, police show vs. melodrama, young vs. middle-aged audiences and similar TV factors, lies a contrast in these two programs that gets to the very core of contemporary network television.

Dallas is a prime-time adaptation of the soap opera mode that goes back beyond the roots to television to radio and excerpted publications of novels in the 19th century. The crucial elements here are a continuing story or plot line, and acting that makes the all-important plot believable. As a daytime vehicle, the soap opera is designed to enthrall viewers in a story that airs five times a week and moves with a speed so imperceptible that a week's or even a month's series of programs can be missed without any harm to the following of the story. The evening transplantation via *Dallas* — and innovative NBC programs such as *Hill Street Blues*, *St. Elsewhere*, and most recently *LA Law* — features filmic (rather than video) treatment of a continuing story broadcast only once a week. Such programs have been enormously successful, and have usually trounced the more conventional types of evening TV with no continuing plot lines.

Enter *Miami Vice*, with neither continuing plot line nor great acting. Indeed, the dialogue — the main means for conveyance of plot — is on *Miami Vice* a fraction of what it is in other TV programs, especially the evening continuing stories. This is because the dialogue is designed not to convey a story in itself, but to contribute in a musical way to the general environment which conveys not so much a story but an impression, and via a variety of sensory modalities.

A typical *Miami* scene shows Tubbs and Crocket — the protagonist detectives — driving down the road, to the accompaniment of a Phil Collins or Glenn Frey recording. Jan Hammer, the musical driving force in the the production, had the script and the images in front of him when he decided just where to put in the music. The result is a multi-dimensional ballet, in which the words of dialogue drop into the scene as almost a spoken lyric in counterpoint to the lyrics of the recording and the visual images. In this context, a mere spoken "yeah" resonates with the impact of an instrument in an orchestration.

Thinness or even total lack of plot becomes about as relevant a criticism of *Miami Vice* in these circumstances as lack of consonance to everyday reality is criticism of an impressionistic or abstract painting. Indeed, if *Dallas* is a Constable — or perhaps a Rubens of TV — then *Miami Vice* is surely a Degas or a Toulouse-Lautrec, sometimes maybe even a Picasso, in its texture. If such comparisons seem extravagant, bear in mind that much of the popular culture of Impressionism was scorned at as cheap commercial art in its time, as some abstract art still is today.

Impressionism was a rare example of what Hegel referred to as the "spirit of an age" — an attitude towards life reflected in many or all modes of expression including painting, poetry, and music. Since the days of Degas, Debussy, and Baudelaire we have not often had such unity in diversities of expression. The psychedelic era of the 1960s held brief promise for such a fusion in music and film, but leached away in a miasma of drugs.

An interesting consequence of *Miami Vice* is the impact it has had in non-televised popular culture, especially music recording. Since the decline of the great creative groups such as the Beatles in the 1960s, music has been obliged to look outside of music for its most exciting developments. The advent of videos álà Michael Jackson earlier in the '80s is credited with rousing the music industry from a ten year slumber. Now artists like Collins and Frey find their most enduring and successful expressions as part of the environment of *Miami Vice*. Songs that are nothing-special love songs when heard "naked" on the radio take on new luster when mixed into the images and dialogue of *Miami Vice*.

Art and television make strange but fertile bedpartners.

IS LAW THE ULTIMATE ETHIC?

What exactly occurred in the Iranian-arms-for-hostages/Contras deal?

A worst case scenario: large amounts of arms were sold to a nation which, although not in a state of war with us, is certainly not our friend. Money from these sales was given to groups opposing the Communist regime in Nicaragua. These actions were taken without Congressional consent or even knowledge, and indeed contrary to Congress' express injunction on supplying funds to the Nicaraguan Contras.

In an atmosphere in which the contamination of Watergate will likely be felt at least through the turn of the century, such events quite understandably raise everyone's hackles. The media, who rightfully see themselves as the heroes of the Watergate affair, are quick to publicize and probe what might be another such event. Elected officials raised in an era of televised Watergate hearings in which assertiveness towards a morally corrupt President and his minions was the hallmark of the good versus ineffective politician strain to outdo each other in their challenges to Reagan to come clean and tell the whole story. The country is abuzz with a déjà vu type of anticipation, and people who never liked Reagan in any case are champing at the bits.

But how similar is the current event, even its worst contour, to the shame of Watergate:

1. Watergate cut to the very heart, not so much of our democratic process of governance, but of our democratic process of election — the very ability of citizens to elect other citizens to office. The Iranian Arms Deal affair has no such ill effect on the election process.

2. Watergate was essentially an activity of self-perpetuation and aggrandizement on the part of the President and his associates (i.e., assure continuance in office.) No such self-benefit seems to have been operating in the Iranian Arms Deal.

3. Watergate entailed an extensive deliberate cover-up by the President and his associates. Thus far — as far as we know — no cover-up of such magnitude is taking place in Washington.

So why is everyone so upset?

Well, the specter of either (a) a President so out of touch that the Iranian Arms Deal events could have happened without his knowledge, or (b) a President who either by design or implication went against the wishes of Congress is certainly not comforting. But neither do these events add up to the fundamental perversion of democracy that was the flashing red light message of Watergate.

In the end, Watergate horrified even many of Nixon's supporters, because the stinginess and paranoia of spirit it bespoke was an affront to anyone other than a thorough-going totalitarian. Watergate was an attack on our democratic system in ends as well as means.

But for those who do not condemn or scoff at the Contras' cause, how much umbrage can be felt for a plan that put the Ayatollah's money behind the anti-Sandinista effort? If we agree with the motive and goals of the Arms Deal plan, all that we can reasonably condemn is the breaking of law the implementation of this plan may have entailed.

Now subversion of the law, especially by government officials, is a serious matter indeed. But are we a nation of laws to such an extent that no laws are worth bending or breaking in pursuit of a higher ethical motive?

Consider the following: Shortly before US entrance into World War II, a boatload of Jewish refugees from Nazi Germany showed up at a US port. Adhering to the law, US immigration officials dutifully turned the boat away — and back to Europe, where most of the Jews on board wound up in concentration camps. Would anyone care to argue that breaking the law on this occasion would not have been the best course of action?

The moral issues of the Iranian/Contra events are certainly not on a par with those concerning Nazi Germany. But neither ought we ignore these issues when judging Oliver North and company. The ultimate hero in national and international events is surely not one who merely follows the law.

HOSPITAL MEDIUM

Strange places, hospitals are. Somewhere between one of Dante's circles and the bridge of the Starship Enterprise, they seem to represent the very most that technology can do for people. In these buildings, aspects of life seem both unreal and far more vivid than they do on the outside, as humans come face to face with monitors, blades, and gadgets of all sorts that deliver and save life, or do quite the opposite.

The highness of the stakes and the general incomprehensibility of the gadgetry coaxes most people to abdicate part of their responsibility and control, and meekly or grumblingly do as they are told. Time enough to question or complain after you have been saved.

There is indeed a bizarre, wry comedy in this place. It is unfortunately not just a bad joke that nurses come into your room at five in the morning to ask if you are sleeping well — or that some worker arrives to install a TV set just as you are about to step into a shower.

Still, it is hard to be too angry. For one, this place holds your loved ones hostage, and you dare not be too angry, even to yourself, lest your anger in some mystical way get back to those in control.

More positively, the hospital does by and large secure and safeguard life. With all the indignities small and large, the stay in the hospital often results in an enhancement of the greatest dignity of all: living, loving beings.

And isn't this, in more diffuse and multi-dimensional form, exactly what occurs in our relationship with technology in the world at large? We suffer the indignities of traffic jams, poor telephone connections, slowness on computer databases — all because these devices nonetheless enhance and expand our living relations, bring us into closer contact with other human beings.

Three years ago, when I left the hospital with Tina and our new-born son Simon in our arms, I felt like we were escaping from Alcatraz. As we went down in the elevator and walked through the lobby out the front door, I was figuratively ready to deliver a karate chop to anyone who interfered.

This time, as we escaped with our new-born daughter Molly, I must admit that I felt a little better. Perhaps, as we walked from the technological microcosm into the technological world, I finally came to realize that, much as I would like our babies to be born in private uncomplicated surroundings — much as I would wish our world to be all trees and flowers and soft breezes — we need more than a dollop of the artificial, of the public intrusion, to make these gifts possible.

COUNTING SHEEP IN SEPIATONE

Well, I must admit Bogey's blue suit looked atrocious in the "colorized" *Maltese Falcon* I saw on TV last week. Then again, the colorizing wasn't intended for those of us who, like me, grew up on black-and-white Bogey on Channel 11 lateshows here in New York — not not to mention the several generations my senior for whom the silver screen was far more than a metaphor.

The controversy over colorizing of 1930s and '40s movies originally filmed in black-and-white has all the earmarks of a classic put-upon artist versus commercial philistine confrontation. Like the once shining art nouveau and deco buildings now eyed by hungry real estate developers, the nearly orphaned black-and-white movie classics seem easy prey to hot-shot distributers bent on making a quick colorized buck. Yet the object of the new coat of paint is to make the old movies more attractive to younger audiences — and is not appreciation by future generations one of the goals of all art?

Why did color motion pictures supplant black-and-white in the first place? Humans always opt for more natural media when given half a chance. In our original need to communicate beyond the biological constraints of vision, hearing, and memory, any medium — however distortive — was welcome. But as our technological prowess matured, we insisted on voices rather than dots and dashes in our long distance interaction, and on motion, sound, and color in our photographic records and narratives. The fact is that we see in color not black-and-white in the real world, and generally see with some sort of accompanied sound, which is why black-and-white and silent movies fell by the wayside. At the same time, still photography and blind radio survive and flourish, because stillness and sound without vision are important parts of our real-world perception — mountains and most far away objects are still, and the world grows dark every night but never really silent. Still photography and radio have thus attained human ecological niches — by replicating human patterns of perception — whereas black-and-white and silent photography did not. (See my "Human Replay: A Theory of the Evolution of Media," Ph.D. dissertation, NYU, 1979, available in bound photocopy from University Microfilm Inc., Ann Arbor, Michigan, for more.)

The other side of the coin, though, is that human creativity is wonderful at making the most out of limited technologies — of making a virtue out of a media vice. A full-fledged silent movie seen in a proper context is quite an experience in liquid sculpture — nothing at all like the idiotic snippets of Keystone Kops that most people take for the silent era — and an occasional film historian can still be heard to lament the advent of talking heads over the evocative silent ballet that reached its height with Griffith in the Teens, and Eisenstein, Fritz Lang, and others in the Twenties.

Does the same hold true for black-and-white movies? No doubt that John Huston and the great directors made deliberate use of the special contours and shadows and effects afforded by the shaded scenario. No doubt that black-and-white, like any limited medium, gives the mind's eye a bit more room in which to roam. But was or is the non-color or color of a film really essential to its appreciation — or constitutive of its existence in the fundamental way that dialog or lack of is? How much of the hullabaloo over black-and-white is obstinate nostalgia — clinging to the fountain pen of one's youth, when the ballpoint, the felt-tip, and successors have long been doing the job much better?

I prefer Bogey in slate to blue, sure. But his charm lay in the way he somehow managed to be convincing through his rattled lines, and this will likely continue to come through whatever the color of his suit or our memories.

SEARCHING... VIA COMPUTER
AND PAPER AND PEOPLE

How helpful are computerized searches in location of scholarly sources and citations?

When I returned from Cape Cod this past September, I had 17 incomplete citations out of a 400-plus bibliography for my *Mind at Large*. The manuscript was already late for the publishers, so I had less than no time to track these down.

I immediately instituted a multi-pronged campaign, including data-base searches, in-person library visits, student slave labor, and calls to relevant people to obtain this information.

I retrieved two citations via Compuserve's Iquest (which hooks into Dialog at very inexpensive rates, and charges you for hits or successful discoveries only — not for time spent online) instantly. These were articles written by Stephen Jay Gould and published in *Paleobiology*. Since I was able to specify the author and publication, retrieval of the titles was a cinch.

In two other cases, I knew the general title of the book and part of the author's name. These were retrieved pretty quickly from Iquest's scanning of *Books in Print*.

Prime lesson in computerized searching: the more you know about your quarry, and the more recent its vintage, the easier it is to discover. (This is the case to some degree in all kinds of searching — but as we'll see below, online searching is particularly vulnerable to not having at least a piece of the exact title already at hand.)

My trips to the physical library were fruitful in a different way. I remembered reading about a book (I think in the *NY Times Book Review*) several years ago that discussed the way the emigration of scientists to England and America from Germany in the 1930s changed the evolution of science by placing these scientists in environments which encouraged their work in unexpected ways. However, I hadn't the faintest recollection of the title or author of this book. Searches of the online *Books in Print* gave me lots of titles about German emigration and German scientists, but none about both (I did find an interesting work about German intellectual emigration to America in the 1840s....) The in-person card catalog listed an out-of-print book, *The Muses Flee Hitler*, that was definitely not the book I had read about. But the book was fascinating and valuable in its own right, and I was happy to substitute this book for the one I originally wanted to cite, and to elaborate my footnote with the material from the *Muses* volume.

Within three days, my various modes of investigation had reduced my outstanding incomplete citations to: one. But this was a toughie.

Back at the beginning of the year, someone had told me about an article in the *Wall Street Journal* in which the author opined that electronic storage of information would replace paper about as soon as computers would replace bathroom tissue. I needed to cite this wrongheaded (the physical texture of paper, essential to its use in the bathroom, has little to do with its capacity for information storage) but colorful view as an example of the stubborn attachment that so many of us have to the thinly-sliced tree as a communications medium.

I scanned the *Wall Street Journal*'s online index. Several articles on the paperless office, on paper and computers, on the future of information storage, but none even vaguely resembled the toilet paper story. Perhaps the article had appeared someplace else (in *Better Homes and Gardens*?). I came up with more than 25 stories on our paperless future and its likelihood, but none on the bathroom connection.

I was getting desperate already. Students were driving me crazy in my online course (which I had neglected just a bit — ever notice how just when you need to do something else, that's exactly the time when everyone else with any justification requires your immediate attention?), my editor was on the phone demanding the manuscript (which was originally promised for May 1), and I couldn't track down this one last citation. I sent out my best student research assistant to the library. "Don't call me again until you find this citation," I told her as gravely as I could. "It's just not there, Professor," she called me the next evening.

I sat with the manuscript in front of me. Four years of work, as complete as I could make it, with the exception of this one maddening citation. I entertained and rejected — as always — the possibility of taking out this citation altogether.

I called my editor and told him the manuscript would be in his office later in the day. Then I found myself calling the *Wall Street Journal*, and explaining my problem to the person who answered.

They found my story in two minutes ("Paperless Office?", *Wall Street Journal*, February 27, 1986). It was sitting in a file of paper clippings under the topic "Paperless Office." The editorial assistant I had contacted had remembered the story.

But it wasn't really a full fledged article or story at all, which is why it had not been recoverable by conventional search modes. The title was really a subtitle in a Business Briefs column — and thus the title could have been recovered only via an enormously expensive full-text (rather than title and author) search. (Alas my research assistant, who might have seen the subtitle on microfiche, had been looking for titles too.)

Paper in a clippings file ... an editorial assistant's recollection ... a lot to be said for people over computers after all — *if* you can get people to talk to you.

FLIPPED-OUT PRIVACY
AND THE TELEPHONE

Marshall McLuhan, with customary wit and insight, was fond of pointing out that the North American goes out to be private, because the inside of most North American homes is public. By this McLuhan meant: the traditional home as castle crumbles when the castle walls admit all manner of electronic transmissions, including television and most especially telephone. On the other hand, the outside from an informational point of view is much more protected and private: people can't talk to you when you're walking in the street without your first seeing them and therein admitting them (or not) to your informational audience.

Telephones are especially telling in the dissolution of privacy in the home, for their rings carry the cachet of a real person immediately at hand on the other end who cannot be ignored. The telephone is thus a medium you cannot easily say no to, regardless of what you may be doing, and we theorists of technology who have carefully studied the matter have long been aware of the "telephonus interruptus" phenomenon, ultimate testament to the telephone's power.

Telephone answering machines partially address the intrusive ring, providing for the telephone what the window shade does for the window: both interdict the respective acoustic and visual Peeping Toms that the telephone and first window brought into being. Still, the answering machine creates new anxieties: who would let a machine answer a call when an *important* call of some sort is expected?

Personal computers can further de-privatize the home, though in a manner far more controllable than the telephone. For the workaholic, a computer at home is a dream come true. How else can you not only compose at two o'clock in the morning, but get your compositions to within keystroke reach of its intended victims on a public computer bulletin board? I've also got to admit that, although I enjoy aspects of time off and holidays in general, I've also always found them confirmative of the establishment. For someone who wants to make it — who wants to move and change things — hours and certainly days out of the year in which no business can be done are anathema. (See my chronicle "The Cursor and the Moon" for more on my critique of holidays.)

But if our homes are no longer private, where can we be private? Is a walk on the street, certainly not everyone's cup of tea in every big city, our only recourse?

In your automobiles, McLuhan answered years ago — citing the privacy and control that people have in the interior of their cars as one reason why mass public transportation would never replace the American way of travelling.

Of course, those were the days before the mobile cellular car phone. Would I be willing to mortgage this last bit of privacy by buying a mobile phone? You bet I would — as soon as my workaholic ways pay off and I can afford it.*

---

*January, 1992: A friend gave us a mobile phone as a present in 1990. But it's a heavy model, and since we have to lug it between two cars, we rarely use it. On at least one occasion, however, it was more than worth its weight: I was stuck in traffic on my way to deliver a well-paying keynote address to a conference in the Catskills, and the mobile phone allowed me to call my hosts so they could rearrange the schedule with a minimum of inconvenience.

THE SECRET OF STAR TREK

In a world in which personal heroes for many of us and political heroes for all of us come and go faster than a fleeting television series, we fittingly look for comfort and stability in the heroes of our media. Myths sewn and embroidered through centuries were once the sinews of our culture. Now the instant and near-instant reach of television and cinema provide horizontal equivalents of the vertical myth-building process, creating heroes via exposure to millions of minds in days and months where decades and centuries were formerly needed. Still, the rapid pace usually shows, and the horizontal heroes of our electronic century are often thin and unsatisfying. Who cares anymore about Ben Cartwright, or even Luke Skywalker?

Exceptions occasionally arise. James Bond — the man with the golden pun — has entertained us with surprising consistency since the early 1960s, and Perry Mason has returned to television a good deal more believable than in the 1950s. But *Star Trek* and its story may be the most astonishing and enduring of them all.

Its humble and almost humiliating beginnings have justly achieved near fairy-tale status: the prince of thoughtful viewers cancelled by the mean network witch after three short years, to return in the after-life of syndication to become the most culturally significant television series in history. And now the television years, deep and universal in our environment, have become tap roots rich and vast for a film series that has improved to the point of surpassing *Star Wars* (itself greatly influenced by *Star Trek* on TV, not to mention Asimov's *Foundation* and Herbert's *Dune* book series), and the *Next Generation* first-run syndicated television series that boldly flaunts its success in the face of the networks.

The roots of *Star Trek* give it advantages seldom seen in film. Whereas *Star Wars* had to create from scratch or borrow not only its heroes but its context and texture — and ultimately slipped on a carpet insufficiently aged to support the intended profundity of the trilogy — *Star Trek* films grow generally better with each release, sustained by a background of characters and detail that we know so long and well as to take for a real history of the future, not film.

I first met *Star Trek* when my wife was just my girlfriend and both of us were students in City College. This afternoon we took our two children to see the latest *Star Trek* movie.* What else comes close to providing this sort of home base against which to measure our progress in life? Rock 'n' roll gives us something of this, but in a more static way, for to hear the Beatles today is to hear the Beatles yesterday, and not at all the way they might sound today.

Media draw great strength from hybridizations with other media — film borrowing from theater, and TV from the conventions and structures of film and radio. The hybrid energy of *Star Trek* is boosted by yet another factor: not only do the films borrow from TV, but the whole enterprise (small and capital) borrows and builds upon itself. The knowledge that everyone has about this 23rd/24th century universe from the TV series and the earlier movies serves as an expanding source of small jokes, visual puns, knowing glances, and all that in turn help us know the characters even better in subsequent movies. In such a hypercycle, even a bad movie (such as the first *Star Trek* motion picture) altruistically works to increase our belief.

Meanwhile, we move closer to a *Star Trek* society in our own reality. I doubt that we'll ever find a planet Vulcan, but who doubts that someday a real Starship Enterprise will be searching the heavens for life, propelled in profound ways by the Enterprise on the screen in the 20th century?

The ultimate accomplishment of *Star Trek* may be the real cosmic civilization that its popular culture someday helps bring into being.

---

*January, 1992: The movie referred to here was *Star Trek IV*. Last week our family went to see *Star Trek VI*. And we eagerly watch every new episode of *Star Trek: The Next Generation* on TV — the only TV program that our whole family regularly watches together.

THE NETWORKS AND AIDS

Nothing should come between a network and its audience during the act of broadcasting. —Dennis Miller, *Saturday Night Live (Comedy Show) NBC-TV, January 25, 1987,* commenting on the continuing refusal of TV networks to broadcast public service announcements and commercial advertisements for condoms, as recommended by Public Health officials for prevention of the spread of AIDS.

The saddest part of Miller's incisive joke is that the networks' resistance to the broadcasting of condom announcements is doing to the American public precisely what Miller's metaphor implies.

Television since its inception as a mass medium in the late 1940s has been the most prudish medium in America — this despite TV's well-earned reputation as a panderer to public tastes for quick sex and violence. The sexual revolution in media begun by *Playboy* in the 1950s and movies like *I Am Curious Yellow* in the 1960s somehow never made it to television. For one, television is obliged — unlike magazines and movies — to broadcast in the "public interest" (as defined and scrutinized by the FCC). Second, as a mass commercial medium of simultaneous national proportions, television has always followed a fundamental principle of being at all costs offensive to no one — far better to bore a sophisticated viewer in New York or LA than horrify an upstanding citizen in Topeka or Peoria. The result of this unholy alliance between government-defined public interest and sponsor-supported inoffensiveness has been a TV content that perpetually titillates but reveals neither flesh nor truth in most instances. You'll see the tightest jeans and slickest news headlines imaginable on network TV: but never the derrière and rarely the full stories behind these. (Ted Koppel's *Nightline* is a notable partial exception in the news category.)

The condom controversy, however, may at last be splitting this alliance, pitting clear public interest against presumed sponsor sensibilities. Let's face it, no one likes condoms. They are an unwelcome responsibility, a deliberate act of logical intervention, at times when the burden of rationality is the last thing on our minds. With the sharp reduction of venereal disease (the original purpose of the "prophylactic" condom) and advent of the pill and other birth control devices in the 1960s, the condom was gladly consigned to the role of scenic detail in films about the '50s and earlier times (such as Mike Nichols' *Carnal Knowledge*). But the recent advent of an invisible sexually transmitted killer with a shelf life of five to ten or more years has given the condom new, undeniable cachet: as AIDS spreads through the population, the illogic of unprotected sex with a casual partner should outweigh the inconvenience of condom usage. Indeed, this is probably already the case, and so one must ask: is the networks' concern over the feelings of some of its viewers and hence its sponsors worth the loss in lives that lack of condom use will likely entail?

The TV networks are not the only institution embroiled in the condom issue. The Catholic Church, long an opponent of condoms due to their (artificial) birth control effects must similarly ask itself: is the increase in life that may result from unmechanically-chaperoned sex worth the loss in life from AIDS that lack of condoms may cause?

But the Church does not generally use public airwaves, and is intended to operate in an interest much higher than the public's. The brunt of the condom problem thus falls to the networks, and I recommend the following: that the FCC immediately move to strip any TV station and/or network of its license if it refuses to broadcast ads for condoms. I do not relish seeing an ad for condoms in the middle of *Miami Vice* — even the fallen New Yorker that I am — and certainly could think of better viewing for my young children. But these are matters of taste, and AIDS is a matter of death.*

---

*January, 1992: I am glad to see that condom ads have begun to occasionally appear on some television stations. But they still don't appear often enough, and on enough stations. And, for such ads to be effective, the condom should be linked to sexual prowess and pleasure in the way that perfumes and the like are so tantalizingly advertised on TV.

TRAINING FOR THE FUTURE

I'm writing this on a Radio Shack M100 laptop computer, which is in turn on an Amtrak Metroliner train hurtling south with me just above Philadelphia to Washington. I'm on my way to give a paper about online communication to a massive in-person conference on technological literacy, and I took this mode of 19th century transport in the hope of getting a bit more perspective on our technological revolutions.

The train is two hours longer than the plane, but in almost every other respect seems a superior way to travel:

ENTRY: I had some business to attend to in New Jersey this morning, so I caught the Metroliner at Newark's Penn Station. No Victoria Station in London, to be sure — or even Grand Central in its heyday in New York City — but a lot more charming, and easier to navigate, than any airport terminal. No huge corridors to run down, no metal detectors, no terrorists or hijackers to worry about. And the train left precisely on-time.

THE RIDE: Travelling more than 100 miles per hour on a ground level contraption is not the most comfortable experience in the world. Indeed, the plane is much smoother — physically. But here's the rub for the plane: I actually find the feeling of not moving, when I know I'm moving very fast (as in a plane) somewhat disconcerting psychologically. Similarly, the unevenness of the fast train is oddly comforting — creating intangible kinesthetic feelings that somehow mesh well with what I see and what I know to be happening. So the bumpy train ride beats the formaldehyde-smooth plane ride in my book at least.

PERIPHERALS: The food on the train is much better, the railphones (which allow phone connection to anyplace in the US — next time I take Amtrak I'm going to try and upload one of these Chronicles) are inexpensive and clear, and I like the way the guy comes around and looks at my ticket. (For some reason, this guy looks the same to me on most of the trains I've taken. I have a theory about this now: the guy looks the same because he IS the same: the train industry quietly mastered cloning some time ago, or is populated by groups of benevolent, highly courteous aliens who look alike.)

The view of many critics of our technological society that new devices obliterate older devices and thereby deprive us of real choice is only partly correct. New machines indeed tend to make older modes less accessible, but in most cases the older modes continue on in some form or another for a very long time. And this gives us a continuing option to renew them if they have value beyond mere nostalgia.

A century after the invention of the typewriter, some people still continue to do most writing by hand. A decade after the introduction of word processing finds a goodly number of writers on the immediate print-on-paper typewriter. Neither of these techniques makes much sense to me, but I recognize their continuance as vivid examples of the durability of older technological ways.

The train has similarly survived the advent of both the car and the plane. (Though alas, not everywhere — the replacement of the Cape Cod railroad and its spectacular lake views with a bike trail is a creative though nonetheless regrettable loss.) For the middling distance to travel — the few hundred miles too long for the car and too short for the plane — the train may be the best form of transport yet developed. People in Europe and Japan already understand this. I expect the tenacity of the rails to make a crucial contribution to the development of this planet in the next century.

MULTI-TASKING
AND THE HUMAN JUGGLER

One of the most exciting developments in personal computing is "multi-tasking": micro-computers capable of doing lots of tasks at the same time. Imagine being able to telecommunicate one document, print out another, and compose a third on the same machine all at once. Actually, print buffers and spoolers have freed computers for other tasks while printing for quite some time, and several telecommunications programs that allow the computer to perform other functions while communicating have been available for a while. But genuine, full-fledged multitasking would make these steps towards simultaneity seem but the first moves in an infant's crawl.

The human being has a peculiar penchant for rapidly becoming accustomed to revolutionary technological advances, and thirsting mightily for more. Automobiles that travel 50 mph are much faster than common horse transport, and yet the quest for cars that moved faster than 100 mph was already felt — and expressed in a variety of cars — as early as the 1920s and '30s. Computers from a decade ago that operate at 2.5 MHz are lightning fast compared to any mechanical writing or filing device, and yet this speed is now unbearably slow to anyone doing a large writing or filing job on a computer. The machine that can do only one job at a time — however marvelously —will likely similarly become intolerable precisely because it whetted our appetites for data magic.

Multi-tasking also is appealing because human beings seem to be inherently multi-tasking creatures. Our imaginations always outstrip our actual productivity, and leave us perpetually panting to accomplish more. (William James' observation that were it not for our consciousness, the world would be "booming, buzzing confusion" is appropriate here: in evolving to make sense out of a multi-dimensional, fast-moving world, human consciousness comes with the capacity to process a lot of things at once. This is why, by the way, we have little problem dealing with the enormous informational invitations of a library or bookstore — and why I argue that overload is often an illusion, and when not, often a case of not using the information-processing mechanisms we already have at our disposal. See my paper, "Overload as Underload," currently in preparation and to be published sometime in the 1990s.)

Multi-tasking is the secret of radio's survival: television stole radio's content (Jack Benny and *Gunsmoke* jumped from radio to TV), and presented it more effectively (most would agree) with pictures and sound. But TV, like all visual media, requires a degree of attention to be perceived, and thus dominates activities in a way that radio does not. (TV is a lot less demanding in this regard than books, which require not only awakeness but a high degree of mental activity in order to be effectively consumed. The appeal of TV lies in its capacity to be partially snored at — but it nonetheless demands a focus that is unnecessary for the perception of sound-only media. Sound, after all, is intrinsically perceivable whatever the position of the hearer's head.) (See my chronicle "Seeing Edward R. Murrow Now" for more on the undemanding quality of TV and the need this addresses.)

Thus, the incidental, non-dictatorial quality of radio made it an ideal companion for breakfast and drives to work, and indeed people who drive to work are prone to list listening to the radio as one of the main reasons that they would be loathe to switch to public transportation. The public riders, for their part, often say that they value the rush hour ride on the train precisely because it gives them time to read the morning or evening paper. Both represent deep-seated desires for multi-tasking.

The study of technology and its history discloses that the development and survival of media and technologies are more than the haphazard, commercially-oriented affairs that they often are portrayed to be. Technologies rather survive only if they satisfy some human need — achieve what might be called a media ecological niche. Radio survived the rise of TV because hearing without seeing is a feature of human perception and cognition; meanwhile silent movies were all but extinguished by talkies because seeing without hearing is not. (The world grows dark every night, but never really silent; we can close our eyes much more easily than our ears.) (See my chronicle "Counting Sheep in Sepiatone" for more.)

Multi-tasking will soon be standard in computer performance because it speaks to the taste for simultaneous accomplishment that comes pre-wired in our species. Admit it: much as you've enjoyed this essay, don't you wish you could have been paying a bill, driving to work, or who knows, reading a science fiction novel at the same time?

THE FACE BEHIND "AMERIKA"

ABC-TV's seven-part mini-series *Amerika* has committed the two sins of (a) offending most TV critics in America (such as John O'Connor of the *New York Times*), and (b) — far worse — doing rather poorly in the ratings. It will likely go down as an embarrassment for ABC, and a failure in the hope the network had of moving out of last place in the season race for viewers.

But I come not to bury but to praise *Amerika*. For despite its obvious and many flaws, I think aspects of the program and indeed the film as a whole are among the most significant in the history of American television.

The premise — that the Soviets will have conquered America either this year or in the foreseeable future — is of course absurd. Gorbachev's outrage that the film will poison American attitudes towards the Soviet Union is directed against a likelihood only slightly less implausible than the plot of the film itself, and one must wonder what all the fuss in the world community is about. For the film is not really about the Soviet Union or the United Nations (also vilified in the story), but about America itself, and the ever-present possibilities for home-grown totalitarian developments on American soil.

One of the most vivid portions of the story, aired between 10 and 11 PM last Wednesday, depicted an East German-dominated "UN" peace-keeping tank force literally rolling over and crushing a squatter camp of Americans displaced from the city and obliged to live on the outskirts of a farm town. The townspeople, who at first hate the American "exiles," at last take the ragged band of survivors into their homes and hearts as they limp down the street with their bleeding and dying. For some 45 minutes, we see nothing but first tanks and smoke, and then bodies and people and walking. All of this to a moving musical background with little or no dialog. Students of film history will recognize this sort of restraint and non-verbal power as largely missing from movies since Griffith and Eisenstein, and certainly almost entirely on TV.

Politically, one can certainly draw the intended parallels to Czechoslovakia or Afghanistan (where the Soviets have been about as successful as we were in Vietnam). But parallels to right-wing South Africa, and indeed our own country at times, seem even more compelling. In *Amerika*, the massacre of American "exiles" is fomented by a local American official (the local party leader), insecure in his puppet power. In America, an equally despicable and insecure Governor encouraged National Guard troops to fire into a crowd of unarmed Americans some 17 years ago. The murderers of four students gunned down at point blank range at Kent State in June 1970 have yet to be brought to justice.

Since the rise of Hitler in a nation with 50 years of democratic traditions in the 1930s (Germany had been a constitutional monarchy since the 1870s), western democracies have been rightfully haunted by the question of "can it happen here?" The paradox of democracy is that attempts to stifle or crush totalitarian parties run the risk of courting the very totalitarianism opposed (just as the totalitarian Gorbachev plays the paradox of using his non-democratic powers to insist on the democratic initiatives he rightly sees as so valuable in his country).

But media in the West (and perhaps soon in the East) have the capacity when they function well of at least keeping our minds occasionally attuned to these issues. This is what Orwell's implausible but enormously instructive *1984* was all about.

American TV has till now never dealt adequately — indeed hardly at all — with the swing we took towards totalitarianism in the Nixon years: the enemies list, the plotting in the White House against Democrats, the attempt to muzzle the press in the Pentagon Papers case, the Watergate affair, the murders at Kent State....

I wonder if *Amerika*, whatever the intentions of its creators and the superficial promotion of its network, might not be construed as an attempt.

CRITICAL MEDIA COVERAGE
AND GREAT IMPULSE LEADERSHIP

Josh Meyrowitz argues in his *No Sense of Place* that omnipresent media coverage has done away with the political hero: whereas prior to the 1960s, perhaps ending with Kennedy, political leaders could keep their backroom wheeling and dealing secret enough to appear wise or dashing or both to the general public, now the unblinking eye of the television camera shows the people what leaders really are, backroom hesitations and machinations and agonizations and all. Certainly every president since and especially including Nixon has been hurt by media revelation of what went on behind the curtain. But is such coverage really lethal to all political heroes, or only to a certain kind of potential hero whose brooding style is vulnerable to such reporting?

The strong suit of America has always been our penchant for acting or doing first, and then analyzing. Nor is this an anti-intellectual attitude: John Dewey, the quintessential American philosopher, wrote that action and production properly precede reflection and contemplation (or else: what have you to reflect upon), and E. H. Gombrich, the British art historian, is fond of emphasizing that "making comes before matching." The problem with too much analysis before the action is that, in this complex world of ours, the choices are so many that the analysis can go on forever — with the result that the status quo is confirmed and no action takes place.

The last American President who successfully acted on impulse was John F. Kennedy. The down-side of this approach was the Bay of Pigs and the missile build-up. The up-side was people on the moon in 1969, the Peace Corps (expressive of a respected and even loved America in many parts of the world), and a general *joie de vivre* missing in America since Kennedy's assassination in 1963. Kennedy was subjected to plenty of media coverage — not all positive — but his taste for bold public initiatives put him on top of the media much of the time.

Nixon and Carter, whatever their substantial differences in intent and content, were both agonizers and pre-action analyzers. And thus the media — for quite different specific reasons — had field days with both these Presidents, who spent much of their time playing catchup ball with adverse media coverage.

Aspects of Reagan's Presidency captured the (John) Deweyesque-Rooseveltian (TR & FDR)-Kennedyesque tradition of acting first and publicly, capturing the center stage, and then fully discussing (I take this sequence to in many ways be the essence of good leadership). But the Iran-Contra affair showed a different side of Reagan — behind the eight-ball of events, not on top of them, scrambling and even agonizing to come up with a believable position — and this revelation has been the most destructive event in his Presidency.* Of course, in fairness to Reagan, the climate of media criticism is a good deal more vigorous now than it was in the 1960s.

The irony may be that unrelenting media scrutiny — certainly good for democracy in the case of Nixon — may have made totalitarian, media-stifled soil the best place to grow a dynamic, action-first leader. Kris Kristofferson commented that Gorbachev may be the most innovative leader since JFK, and certainly Gorbachev's initiatives in arms negotiations and Soviet domestic matters have captured the world's attention, placed the US in a reactive role, and will likely do the human species much good. One gets the impression that Gorbachev, much like Anwar Sadat who also used a non-democratic, non-critical society as a foundation to do great things, has a talent for dramatic impulses that clear the board of complicating extraneous pieces and often get to the high moral and practical ground.

In view of this, the problem facing our democratic society may well now be: how to maintain our justly cherished open society without inhibiting the impulse to great leadership. How to elect Presidents who don't need to apologize. I have no answers to this problem, but note with concern the field of candidates in the next election.

*January, 1992: George Bush's immense popularity when he acted decisively in the Gulf War, and equally immense decline in the wake of his perceived indecision regarding the economy, continues this pattern.

THE NINE LIVES
OF ELECTRONIC TEXT

Discovery of correspondence stored on an electronic mail system used by Oliver North and his colleagues — IBM's PROFS system — set the stage for a reversal of the traditional concern about the durability of electronically stored information: whereas until recently the main fear of computer users was that electronically encoded data was more easily lost than print on paper, now some people worry that electronically committed information may be far more difficult than paper to adequately dispose of.

Most computer users are unaware of the profound differences between the erasing or deletion of information on paper and the deletion of information in electronic systems — an unawareness which can have surprising consequences, advantageous and otherwise. When one takes an eraser to pencilled scribbling on paper, the information in that scribbling is gone (unless the original pencil inscription was so penetrating as to make an impression on a sheet of paper underneath); information written or printed on paper physically destroyed (via shredder, flame, etc.) is similarly gone with the wind, unless a copy was deliberately made previously. Not so with electronic inscriptions. Consider the following:

1. The routine "Delete" or "Erase" command on most personal computers does NOT erase the file at the time the command is given. What the command in fact does is remove the internal marker of the "erased" file, opening that portion of the disk to re-write by new information or a new file. The original "erased" file no longer shows up on standard disk directories (or searches to see what is stored), and so one behaves as if the file is indeed gone. In actuality, the "erased" file will (a) remain intact on the disk forever if nothing further is written on the disk, or (b) be capable in principle of lasting a long time, depending upon how frequently this disk is "written to" subsequent to the "erasure," and the luck of where on the disk the word-processor randomly deposits new information.

Many simple programs are available for recovering files whose markers have been deleted but whose text is still intact. I've literally restored text more than two years old — thought to be dead and gone until I realized what was going on — via one of these programs.

2. Most computer networks like PROFS have commands that delete comments and messages. In fact, the commands put the "deleted" items in a "queue" where they must wait their turn for actual deletion from the system. Since the comments or messages no longer are accessible to the user via standard display and search procedures, the user assumes the items are gone. In reality, they continue to be retrievable via a variety of means until their turn comes in the debarking line. (North's problem was that the PROFS system he used was specifically designed by IBM to maximize this type of "unconscious" retention of information.)

3. Now here is a really wild situation: You're writing with your wordprocessor. For whatever reason, you accidentally delete everything you've written. Then to your horror you discover that you desperately need this material. But it hasn't been saved anywhere as a file, so the recover procedures discussed above are of no avail. Your information is lost, right?

No:

Anytime you do anything through or with your personal computer, an "image" of all operations — including text typed — is kept in your micro's RAM (the random access memory which is the lobby to all computer functions). Moreover, this image remains in your computer's RAM until you shut the machine off (turn off the power completely). Other operations — loading of new programs, warm and cold boots, etc. — may slightly change the contents of the RAM, but rarely enough to damage the text stored there beyond recognition and retrieval.

The upshot: programs exist that can "dump" or record the complete or partial contents of any RAM to a standard disk file, where they are displayable and editable via standard word-processors, etc.

Features such as these have been embedded in computer systems since their inception, rendering the general perception of computer data as less reliably stored than paper data something of an illusion. As word of the illusion spreads, much of the almost carefree abandon that some bring to computer communication may evaporate. For others, the price of technical illusion may prove as costly as the political kind.

REFLECTIONS ON "BABY M":
PART 1: BEYOND THE DEVIL
AND THE DEEP BLUE SEA

Yesterday's decision in a Bergen County, New Jersey courtroom to give custody of "Baby M" to her biological father and adoptive mother (and not to her biological-surrogate mother — the woman who gave birth to her) clearly draws the line on this question of technology and life between the law and the Catholic Church, which earlier last month decreed that any procreation outside of sexual intercourse was immoral. Though philosophers of technology — and likely most people — will find much to dislike on both sides of the argument, we can all at least be happy that our legal and religious institutions are at last beginning to pay some serious considerations to advances in technology which in the past few decades have radically transformed the very bases of our existence.

The irony of the Church's position has not gone unnoticed even by its highest pastors. In New York City, outspoken Cardinal John O'Connor remarked that after years of preaching against sex without procreation, the Church was now foreclosing the obverse possibility of procreation without sex. Perhaps the Cardinal thinks this not ironic but appropriately complementary. In any case, the Church's reaction, as almost always, to new technological possibilities which by their nature and newness raise profound ethical issues is to say we ought not get involved with these technologies. This may be ethically comforting on some level. But in view of the unsatisfactory status quo — the many people unable to have children via natural intercourse — the Church's new council is discomforting and inhumane on many other levels.

On the other side of the street, the decision of Judge Harvey Sorkow in Hackensack yesterday that a contract is a contract — and must be enforced even when the product is a human being — falls to a new level of dehumanization of its own. True, biological mothers give up forever their children when adoption is finalized, but most states (including New Jersey) are strict about giving the biological mother one last chance to change her mind after the baby is born, regardless of contractual arrangements made previously. This seems an eminently reasonable allowance, and one which Baby M's biological mother was not allowed.

Courts of law, alas, are not the best places for consideration of such fine and profound ethical issues. In the Baby M case, the personality of the biological mother (the Judge cited her as "manipulative" and not believable) apparently played a major role in the decision against her claim. Yet clearly there are principles here which transcend the personalities of the parties involved.

Neither, unfortunately, is the Church the ideal vehicle for policy on these issues. The notion of a group of thinkers, however well meaning, above and beyond us, separated from us, making decisions that we are obliged to follow went out with Plato — though we see strange variants of this notion yet at work in totalitarian societies and in various Churches. A democratic, genuinely participatory society needs more.

The usual trajectory in these matters starts with the use of a new technology and procedure, which continues and expands until it pitches us right in the middle of a painful ethical quandary. Artificial insemination worked — and works — when the inseminated mother is also the adoptive mother. For here we have no conflict between circumstances of conception and social reality of motherhood.

The system breaks down when the biological father claims custody against the wishes of the inseminated mother. Solutions to the effect that no artificial insemination is moral (the Church's) and a contract is a contract (the Baby M Court) are equally unsatisfactory.

In my next Chronicle, I'll outline some approaches that strike me as more responsive and progressive.

REFLECTIONS ON "BABY M":
PART 2: THE BIOLOGICAL REALITIES
OF MOTHERHOOD

On a personal level, I can think of few things as wrenching and revolting and just intrinsically wrong as a judge bloodlessly deciding that a mother may never again see her baby because she had earlier entered into a contract of whatever sort. Were I Governor of New Jersey — or a person with the proper power — I'd institute impeachment proceedings for the Judge, restore the baby to her mother, countermand the rushed adoption proceedings that took place immediately after the trial, and then gladly stand trial myself for whatever infractions I may have committed in so quickly setting aside the Judge's actions. All of which give ample reasons why I'll never be Governor.

But a just society must do more than respond from personal emotion, however right that personal emotion may seem. Personal emotions differ in well meaning individuals, and thus society must strive for a more rational basis of decision.

But what? How are we to make rational decisions in a world in which technology daily transforms the very foundations of logic and common sense and perception upon which we are prone to make our best judgements? In a constantly changing world courtesy of technology, where are we to find bedrocks and standards?

Religion is one candidate for such a role, but as I indicated in my last Chronicle, I find religion often too out of touch with reality to serve as a dependable balance in technological affairs. Although I'm the happy parent of two children produced in the natural, time-honored way, I can't abide a Church that would confine the blessings of parenthood to only those capable of natural procreation (or those willing to adopt a child not of their procreation). If we've learned nothing else as a species, we've presumably learned that we operate best when we apply our technologies to reducing the natural deficiencies of hunger, disease, death, and the like; inability to procreate seems fully in place on this list of things we ought to try to improve upon.

So what, then, are we to base an ethics of technology upon? My candidate is biology — more fully, the biological facts of life.

Let me explain by giving an example, ironically, from religion. Orthodox Judaism has a very interesting way of determining whether a person in question is or is not Jewish: the father's religion is entirely irrelevant; only the religion of the mother counts. Why? Because people will be people, and always have been, throughout the ages, and so Orthodox Judaism recognizes that the putative father may in fact not be the biological father. About the biological mother — the woman who bears the child — there can be no question: she is, whatever her personality and contractual commitments, indisputably the mother. (In our current age of in vitro conception, the mother who bears the child may not be the DNA or genetic mother — the original source of half the life material that will become the baby. Even so, the mother who gives birth has nurtured and in this sense mothered the developing baby in the most intimate way possible for nine months.) Even the genuine biological (DNA) father can make no such claim — and in vitro possibilities notwithstanding, the biological father is intrinsically more difficult to definitively specify than the biological mother.

What possible guidelines can this give us for the Baby M case? Personalities and enforceabilities of contracts aside, we have a dispute between the biological mother and the biological father. A Solomonesque decision that somehow awarded joint custody would obviously be preferable if it were workable, and perhaps the Judge and all parties concerned should have strained for the nearly impossible goal of working out a joint custody arrangement (I admit, though, that the question of what effect this would have on the child is very serious).

But what to do in an either/or, mother/father decision? The mother gave birth to this child, of that there is no doubt biologically. The father's sperm was presumably responsible — and I say "presumably" because, although no one has challenged the accuracy of this claim (I certainly am not), there is an intrinsic second-hand, non-eyewitness quality to this claim of fatherhood. How do we know that the mother didn't sleep with someone else during the artificial insemination period (her husband had had a vasectomy in this case, but even so, there are after all other men in the world). My point here is not to cast aspersions on the mother, but to emphasize that mothers have a primary relationship to birthing that fathers — even when progenitors via natural intercourse — simply do not have.

I thus think that in conflicts between biological mothers and biological fathers, mothers must be given certain initial presumptions and privileges — among them the right to retain their babies even if in violation of an earlier contract. I recognize that this by no means answers every question — and even the cleanest principles must admit to exception — but I think recognition of the biological realities of motherhood is a first step towards building an ethics in this area.

NAUGHTY WORDS
AND OBSCENE CENSORSHIP

The modern (= last quarter century's) FCC involvement with possibly objectionable radio first crested with the famous "seven dirty words" case, originating in 1973 with the broadcast of a recorded routine by the same name by comedian George Carlin. The idea of this *schtick* was to think of, and then explain why, certain works are unambiguously obscene. A word like "prick," for example, does not qualify, since one can still (albeit stiltedly) say in any forum, "Gosh, I've pricked my finger." Even "ass" lacks undilutedly naughty pizzazz, since a remark to the effect that someone has a real nice ass could — not likely, but could — mean that the person so described has an attractive donkey. On the other hand, we can all think of words which possess no such saving ambiguity. Carlin's routine details seven of these zingers (he has since expanded this list to the hundreds, by the way). I saw Carlin give a live performance of this on HBO several years ago, and found it hilarious.

Not so amused was a fellow driving down from ritzy Westchester County into Manhattan in 1973. His son was in the front seat along side him, and the radio was tuned to WBAI-FM (a publicly supported non-commercial radio station with a reputation for unconventional broadcasting). Why the gentleman would choose to listen to this station at all with his little boy right next him is an interesting question, but in any case the fellow was outraged when he and his son were treated to Carlin's routine projected with crystal clarity out of the car's speakers. He wrote the FCC, which in turn advised WBAI-FM that such broadcasting was not to its liking.

Now a censure from the FCC is not quite a censor — no one from Washington comes down to the station to pull the plug — but a censure is still a serious matter. For it carries the possibility of trouble at license renewal time. So WBAI protested — all the way to the Supreme Court. The ACLU and even Jimmy Carter joined WBAI in amicus curiae briefs, but the Court upheld the

FCC: radio and TV have special responsibilities, the Court ruled, not necessarily because they use public airways, but because people who tune them in have no way of knowing beforehand just what they will hear or see. With an x-rated movie or *Playboy* magazine, the consumer knows what he or she is getting into. Not so with the penetrating electromagnetic carrier wave, and thus media that use these have special obligations not to offend.

(The Federal Communications Act which brought the FCC into being in the 1930s, by the way, was actually requested by many radio station operators. In those days, so many people had transmitters that the airways were literally clogged — with stations cancelling each other out — and so the radio industry begged the government for some sort of regulation. Little did they realize....)

Recently (1987) the FCC reasserted its stand against obscenity, and — more disquieting for those who dislike government regulation of communication — warned a disk jockey who is explicitly non-obscene (Howard Stern in NYC: often tasteless and vulgar, yes, but not obscene) that his broadcasts are nonetheless border-line objectionable. The worlds of radio and sociology went into a uproar, but the FCC warning remains.

Quite profound issues underlie the commotion and chortling. Obscenity, vulgarity, and blaspheming serve important psychological functions in our lives and societies: if the guy I zap out of a parking space with my little Olds can't curse me out, and thereby relieve some tension, I'm in trouble: he may do something worse. But to the extent that curse words become publicly acceptable, they become stripped of their emotional punch — neutralized, like yesterday's laughable slang (would you like to be called dishy, or even groovy?), and deprived of the very edge that gives them value as a safety valve. This suggests that we all have some legitimate interest in keeping curse words out of common parlance. On the other hand, the prospect of anyone telling us what we can and cannot listen to should offend every Jeffersonian bone in our bodies, physical as well politic. Allowing others to edit our linguistic intake seems too big a price tag for preservation of the emotional kick in obscenity, which is almost never the purpose of the editors anyway.

Ultimately, we ought to be more offended by what the FCC has done than by what the FCC has sought to protect us from. Let the airwaves be free, and we'll figure out a way to protect the emotion punch of a few choice words, thank you. Why, I've a good mind to write those SOBs and....

CAN ONLY ANGELS BE PRESIDENT?

To what extent is omnipresent and omnirevelatory media coverage a benefit and a hindrance to our democratic political system?

A little less than 100 years ago, President Grover Cleveland underwent extensive, life-threatening surgery for cancer of the jaw. The operation was performed on a yacht that wended its way up the East River in NYC to Buzzard's Bay, Massachusetts. Cleveland's mouth was immobilized for months — but the public knew virtually nothing of the cancer, the operation, and Cleveland's eventual recovery.

The public surely has a right to know about the life threatening illnesses of its Presidents and contenders for the Presidency. Mixing just a fillip of morality in with our justified concern about the health of public candidates, we also seem reasonable in wanting to know if those who wish to serve in public office have physically debilitating dependencies on alcohol and other drugs. The media are probably even right in reporting psychological problems such as the mental depression and shock therapy revealed about Tom Eagleton in 1972 — though the view of many historians that Abraham Lincoln suffered from "melancholia" (the 19th century equivalent of manic-depression) gives us something to think about here: had Lincoln's melancholia been known prior to his running for office, and had news of this problem led to his defeat in the election, would we as a country have been better off?

Cases of "pure" (i.e., health-free) morality are more difficult still. Grover Cleveland, ironically, was first elected President amidst rumors (confirmed by him) that he had fathered an illegitimate child. Both FDR and JFK apparently had love affairs, then unreported, while in office: would we as a nation have been better off with the reportage of these affairs, and the consequent possible destruction of those Administrations? Most historians would say no about Roosevelt — our society was greatly enhanced by his Presidency. Historians are less in accord about JFK, but given my advocacy of the space program, Peace Corps, and other JFK initiatives, I certainly would say that a JFK Administration hurt by published reports of his escapades would not have served the country well.

My assessment of JFK could simply be summarized as: I just do not care whom he slept or did not sleep with. These activities had no impact on my life as a citizen of this country and of the world. I care about presidential activities that do have impact on our lives — activities and attitudes that we presumably evaluate when we elect people to this office. I care about making the world safe and stimulating and prosperous for my family and friends. I care about reducing disease, extending our lifespan, and moving our species out to the stars. You have to reach pretty far to tie any of this to the bedmates of a president.

But let's give the dirt-mongers their due, and consider all possibilities. Two perhaps germane concerns about extra-marital affairs and presidential performance come to mind: quality of character and vulnerability to blackmail.

Lying to one's spouse (if such is indeed the case in an affair) is, after all, lying, and not a quality we would want in a leader. On the other hand, I've always admired Bertrand Russell's insistence that the quality of one's ideas not be held hostage to the quality of one's actions. I can say "Don't exceed the speed limit when driving," then get in my car and drive 75 mph. This says something negative about me, but does it invalidate my advice about driving? (The answer would be yes only if my driving 75 mph was indicative of the extreme difficulty that most human beings might have with a slower speed limit.) Will a president who lies in personal life necessarily lie in public affairs? Poetry and melodrama notwithstanding, I see little connection between affairs of the heart and of state. Is there anyone on the face of this earth who has not lied at one time or another in a personal matter, small or large, and does this then make all of us unfit for public service?

Blackmail — or equivalent destructive pressure that could result from personally questionable behavior — is another matter. Yet even here, the blackmail problem arises only insofar as we as a society view a behavior as bad enough to be blackmailed about. Perhaps the very publicity given extra-marital behavior and the like will render it less blackmailable — much as divorce is no longer a fatal skeleton in a candidate's closet.

Ultimately, we need to decide just what qualities are most essential for effective leadership. How high should the qualities of angels be on our list? In terms of goodness and high moral ground, angels rate very well. Of real human experience — of daily struggling to be a decent, ethical being through a flesh that is only selfish in pursuit of its satisfactions — angels know nothing.*

---

*May, 1992: Bill Clinton's survival, as of this date, as the likely Democratic presidential nominee shows that our society may be maturing a bit on this "angelic" issue. At the very least, Clinton has fared better in the wake of personal allegations than did Gary Hart in 1988.

"SGT. PEPPER"
AND THE PRESUMPTION OF GENIUS

June marks the 20th anniversary of the release of the Beatles' *Sgt. Pepper's Lonely Hearts Club Band*. The album has been continuously proclaimed as the greatest rock recording of all time, and continues to raise a bouquet of fascinating questions about the relationship of commercial popular culture and art.

The album has been very significant in my own life, not only as a cherished group of songs indelibly evocative of my world half a lifetime ago, but as the occasion for the development of one of my first theories of the media. I call this theory the presumption of genius.

I was 20 years old when I first heard *Sgt. Pepper*. I already was a devoted fan of the Beatles, and appreciated them not only for their winning tunes and lyrics, but for their startling capacity to change their music with every new release. The harpsichord on *Rubber Soul*, the backwards tape and fuzz guitars on *Revolver*, George Harrison's (subcontinent) Indian music on both those albums had gone far beyond what anyone ever expected of rock 'n' roll music or even folk-rock. But when I first heard *Sgt. Pepper*, it was too much for me.

I remember talking on the phone with my friend Stu Nitekman — we were not only friends, but co-performers in a folk-rock group called The New Outlook, which sang daily in the alcoves at City College (this is what I did rather than attend classes) and had just signed a contract with Atlantic Records (our single, released the year after, sold less than 600 copies). "They've gone off the deep end this time," Stu and I agreed about the new Beatles' album. (Stu has gone on to co-author a book on Scrabble, and have a moderately successful career as a singer of commercials. His name is now Jonathan Hatch.)

I was not really satisfied with this blanket critique of the Beatles, however. Although I knew enough about the history of art and music and film to know that great artists often do (temporarily or permanently) run out of steam, I also recognized the extreme presumption on my part to conclude on the basis of my first few listenings to an album that its creators — whom I admired above all other groups in the rock pantheon — had fallen flat. I decided to try the presumption another way.

Dislike of a given piece of music can logically derive from (a) the objective lack of quality of the music (the assumption in Stu's and my initial reaction), or (b) inability of the perceiver to appreciate the value of the music. Let's say I gave the Beatles the continuing presumption of genius, and took as a starting premise that the fault I found in *Sgt. Pepper* was mine — that the problem I had with the album was not that the Beatles had gone off the deep end, but that they had gone somewhere where I was unwilling or unable (I hoped the former) to follow. What then?

I deliberately listened to the album over and over again — something I would never do for anyone else's music — and lo and behold, after 9 or 10 listenings, I began hearing wonderful things. It started with "A Little Help from My Friends," the most conventional song on the album, and soon I was loving every lick, at first arcane, now suddenly luxuriously accessible, on the album.

So my presumption of genius worked for the Beatles. But what if *Sgt. Pepper* had been their first album, or an album by a group that I and others might not have deemed worthy of this presumption? How many *Sgt. Peppers* have been obliged, like Gray's poor flowers, to blush unseen and waste their sweetness on the desert air?

The riddles of success in popular culture are complex indeed. Newcomers must have just the right mix of cliché and originality to be taken seriously, and once so taken, they can if they have the talent use the momentum of popular culture as a foundation for more fully original creations. The Beatles, I think, had and understood this more fully than any other group in rock history.

The years have been kind to *Sgt. Pepper*. The South Jersey working-class anthems of Bruce Springsteen have an authenticity that neither the Beatles nor Dylan nor for that matter anyone in the '60s ever had, true; but then again, neither is Springsteen ever likely to employ Schubertian strings, dixieland jazz, Indian raga, and dozens of other strains and flavors of music all in one thematic album.

Somehow in that brief period in the late '60s, the whole history of music and poetry opened up to the Beatles, who transformed their impressions into a tiny but remarkably diverse cross-section of this history. In so doing, this first "compact disk" (a product not only of the Beatles, but of their equally gifted producer George Martin) forever and anon undercut the smug assurance of high culture priests that rock music was but a passing rite of adolescence.

Sgt. Pepper was released three years after McLuhan's *Understanding Media*, and two years before people first walked on the moon. Perhaps the lure this music continues to have for me is, after all, a reflection not only of the quality of the music, but of the fact that the music accompanied the coming of age of my generation. Perhaps we are all duck-like in this respect, pre-programmed to become intensely involved with some type of music for a short time in our lives, and then have a special affection for that music evermore. If such is the case, then I feel privileged to have been part of the electric equivalent of the first students who sat in Plato's Academy. But my presumption is that *Sgt. Pepper* will continue to appeal to all who love music well into the 21st century and beyond.

SOCIAL DIMENSIONS
OF ONLINE COMMUNITIES

I was up in Canada to give the Plenary Address on "Social Impacts of Computer Conferencing" at the Second Guelph Symposium on Computer Conferencing earlier this week. I signed on from the College Motor Inn in Guelph several times, but the truth is I was too exhausted from all the personal exchanges to do much writing. Interesting lesson vis-à-vis online communication and travel: however sophisticated the computer technology (and my Radio Shack Lap Top is a simple but quite powerful and effective device), it still depends upon the physical energy of the human who uses it. In my case, the lure and excitement of in-person interaction proved incompatible with online work. I suppose I could have been a drudge and stayed in the hotel room and typed away, but then the in-person interactions would have suffered.

The Guelph Conference itself was wonderful. One of the high points for me was meeting and talking across a table for about 20 minutes with Marc Belanger, a top Connect Ed student I hadn't met in person before. There is a new mode of friendship afoot: the kind that starts with extensive online exchanges, and then expands in due course to an occasional in-person meeting in which both parties already know each other quite well. In almost all cases, the online and in-person relationships are mutually enriching. (One notable exception is disappointment in romantic relationships that start online and raise false expectations about physical appearances — stories of such disappointment abound in the growing lore of online communities. On the other hand, several cases of true online love consummated in offline relationships — including marriage — have been reported.)

Meanwhile, the proceedings of the Conference in Guelph were outstanding and fascinating. As Murray Turoff (creator of the Electronic Information Exchange System, "EIES") often points out, preaching to the already-converted about the value of online communication is a pleasure. People from a variety of would-be, nascent, and slightly more mature online systems and operations were in attendance, and the feeling I got was one of the New World shortly after its initial settlement by the Old: a series of online outposts and colonies, each facing a slightly different but overlapping series of problems, each tied to the Old World (= traditional place-based, book-paced institutions) but also tied to one another on the profound points of common interest in online communities.

The ongoing community of online communicators at Guelph is also worthy of note. Revolutions often occur in places a bit off the beaten track from the establishment (consider: EIES at NJIT not MIT, Connect Ed working with the New School not Columbia, etc.), and here in this quiet, originally agricultural institution about an hour's drive from Toronto, a computer conferencing community flourishes with a rich mixture of online and inperson attributes. (See my Chronicle "OnLine Education and the Castle Walls" for more on revolutions in education beginning in the backwaters.) Although Guelph's COSY system — one of the two or three best computer conferencing systems in the world (analogous to EIES and PARTI) — has a good number of international users, the system is much more an expression of the physical Guelph inperson campus and community (and the inperson campus in turn an expression of COSY) than is the case with most other major online systems. (EIES and even more so PARTI were developed online by geographically diverse people.) For example, students in inperson classes are often asked (by faculty who have been exposed to the value of online education) to continue discussions of issues online, and indeed many of the themes raised in this Conference at Guelph will continue to receive treatment online.

Gail Mercer was kind enough to enter an abstract of my own address to the inperson Conference into a online COSY conference, and I'm appending that abstract to this Chronicle FYI.

Nice to know that nestled in the farmlands of Southern Ontario is a community with eyes to future and the far corners of the world — a community that speaks our language.

Abstract follows:

TITLE: The Plenary Address:
Paul Levinson, "Social Impacts of
Computer-Mediated-Communication"

The seminar began with a discussion of the social qualities of the book versus those of computer conferencing. Reading a book, says Levinson, is (on a personal level) an intrinsically antisocial act which provides no sense of community in the immediate environment of the reader. If we accept a "hypodermic" metaphor of education, where learners are merely injected with information, then books are enough; but if we view education as involving active cognition and critical discussion, then books though valuable are not sufficient. Levinson points out that the early broadcast media of radio and television attempted to rectify the limitation of only being able to reach one person at a time using one book, but that these were still only one-way communications. All the learner could do was receive, and thus radio and television were still insufficient in terms of a full educational system.

Computer conferencing, however, is interactive, and Levinson points out five of its advantages: 1. Computer conferencing has *interactive asynchronicity*. Anticipation and retrospection are often more intense and meaningful experiences than those of the moment, and thus, by not having to respond to comments immediately, our responses can be much more effective and can go beyond the interactivity of face-to-face communication. 2. Computer conferencing allows *greater retrievability of thoughts*. Along with the ability to add comments retrospectively, this feature affords the freedom to do real creative thinking and to weave ideas, which would otherwise be lost, into the fabric of intellectual discussion. 3. Computer conferencing *levels hierarchies*. The subtle forms of intimidation found in such environments as classrooms and offices are eliminated by computer conferencing, and education becomes the discussion, debate, and conflict of ideas rather than the packaging of propaganda. 4. Computer conferencing *overcomes geographic distances* — a factor which becomes especially important as we move up the ladder of education. For those seeking Ph.D.'s, computer conferencing and its capacity to connect the student to the best possible scholar regardless of where he or she is located is more than a convenience and may actually be a necessity. 5. Computer conferencing provides *benefits to disabled people*. The deaf, for example, can now participate at a level of interaction which they have never had before. Furthermore, Levinson states that we are all "handicapped" in that the actualization and implementation of our goals can only be achieved through social interaction — but, by extending our ability to interact, computer conferencing can help remedy this situation.

VIDEOTAPING THE ECOLOGY OF FEAR

Here in the peace of Cape Cod Bay, with two swans at my front door and Peter Cottontail at my back, the ecology of fear that is New York City's subway system is recallable only with the greatest of difficulty. But anyone who has grown up in NYC or regularly ridden its graffiti strewn trains knows that this experience verges constantly on the realization of your worst nightmare. Hot cars, stalls in tunnels, stops missed due to incessant repairs at stations, and always the danger that someone will come out of the shadows to slash your throat for a nickel.

This was the world of Bernhard Goetz, who calmly fired shots into four nineteen year olds who had approached him on a train and requested five dollars. Goetz said he knew by the looks in their eyes and their general demeanor that they meant him harm, and anyone who has lived in New York for any length of time knows exactly what he meant. In fact, the four had criminal records both before and after the Goetz shooting. In fact, they are black — but their being on the receiving end of Goetz's bullets ultimately had little to do with their ethnic membership. It had rather to do with their membership in a class that cuts across the human race and other species: a class known as predators.

Nine days after the shooting, Goetz explained his crime in a much celebrated video interview. Without benefit of counsel, Goetz detailed the pleasure he took at lashing out at his tormentors —how, a victim of a previous mugging, afraid for his life, he coolly meted out punishment to those who he felt were on the verge of doing this to him again. The response of the District Attorney (Robert Morgenthau) — who as part of the law enforcement system in NYC is in my view guilty in some sense for the deplorable condition that Goetz burst out against — the response of this official upholder of law and order was to put Goetz on trial. (I know: no one goes to trial without the finding of a Grand Jury. Yet the DA who initiates the trial process is surely also responsible for bringing innocent people to trial.)

The jury found Goetz not guilty of everything save a gun possession charge. According to his lawyer (Barry Slotnik), the same videotape that so motivated the DA was crucial in portraying to the jurors Goetz's state of mind. A written transcript of Goetz's confession — all that would have been available a few years ago —likely would have convicted him. But the illegally recorded tape captured the fear that led to the shootings; and the jury, like any reasonable people, quite naturally thought about the conditions that generated this fear.

These conditions — and the vagaries of social and political structures (including Transit Police sadly more directed to catching fare-beaters than maintaining safety on the trains) — are the true villains in this story. They and their expression in the four muggers on the train that day are the ones who deserve to be tried and found guilty.

Score one for videotape and our jury system.*

---

*May, 1992: The performance of videotape and jury in the April, 1992 Rodney King verdict is clearly less commendable. On the one hand, the world could see with its own eyes on videotape the continued beating of Rodney King by Los Angeles police officers well after he had been rendered defenseless; on the other hand, jurors looking at this same tape, and having it put into context by defense attorneys, found three of the four police officers innocent of all charges, and were unable to reach a verdict on the fourth. Apparently, in the courtroom, at least, seeing via videotape is not believing — a healthy enough attitude in general given the capacity of audiovisual media to mislead, but also proof that the power of documentary media to promote good by uncovering wrong is only as strong as the minds of the people who see such documentary evidence.

VOULEZ-VOUS CC
AVEC MOI CE SOIR?

Word from France is that that country of *l'amour*, techno-logically backward (at least as far as telephone and telecommu-nications) as recently as the early 1970s, has leapfrogged into a society of love-making via exchanges of electronic text mes-sages, courtesy of the "Minitel" system that put a computer terminal in every home in order to free people from the tyranny of heavy, out-of-date phonebooks.

"Hot chatting," as the French practice has been known in American online circles, has been a feature of virtually every computer conferencing ("cc") system ever invented. Although the faceless romances conducted through words on a computer screen are interesting as a species of sexual activity, they are more interesting for what they reveal about human communication and its attachment to in-person presence. Many of the discoveries in the "rose" (= soft pornography) message boards of Minitel confirm what many us have been observing here on public computer systems in the past few years:

• the lack of personal inhibition in cc situations often leads to more honest ("soul to soul") communications than often found in in-person exchanges;

• online or cc exchanges are often more dignified and literary than spoken exchanges (again, the lack of inhibition stimulates creativity);

• online pseudonyms provide a cover for the most revealing exchanges;

• online friendships and deeper relationships can play dominant roles in the offline lives of the participants.

The big difference between the American and French experiences with cc is that while ours is yet only a fractional subculture of our society, the French online environment is mainstream to the point of becoming French society. Govern-mental officials make pronouncements on Minitel policies, sexually explicit ads for the late-night online rendezvous draw criticism from stodgy elements of the population, *Le Monde* first denounces then embraces lines of text exchanged in the night (if passion pulls us into the 21st century, it has served its purpose... *embracez mon texte*).

Minitel officials worry that all of this textual massaging may be a fad. But media historians know that once a medium gets into a culture's bloodstream, it is all but impossible to expel. Like the printer's ink of the Renaissance, and the sights and sounds of cinema and radio and TV in our own century, the seductive flickers on the 21st century terminal will likely be with us for a long, long time.

How altogether like the charming twists of technological innovation and diffusion that the 21st century of communication has achieved its most humane nation-wide flowering to date in a country which gave us Jacques Ellul, the world's leading critic of technology, and where a National Assemblyman not long ago observed, "Half of France is waiting for a telephone, the other half is waiting for a dialtone."

MEANWHILE,
BACK IN THE MOTHERLAND...

I returned from England last week, filled with enthusiasm about the future of computer conferencing in the Open University, in the United Kingdom, and by extension throughout the world. What prompts this Chronicle, alas, is another event that just happened in England — an event all the more disturbing when considered against the backdrop of the democratic possibilities opened up by online networking.

The event is the Thatcher government's (a) banning of live interviews and direct quotes from terrorists, IRA members, and the like on BBC radio and television, and (b) policy that silence — refusal to speak — can now be deemed evidence of guilt in British courts.

Both of these moves, though no doubt born of understandable frustration in a world plagued by terrorism, are astonishing attacks on the bulwarks of democracy. At a time when the world is being thrilled to the marrow with the first rays of freedom in the Soviet Union, England — the birthplace of modern Western democracy — is taking a frightening step backward.

The move has all the slippery signs of fascism. On *Nightline* the other night, I heard a Thatcher representative smoothly explain that such fundamental rights as refusing to incriminate oneself were sanctified in earlier times, now long past, and no longer appropriate to the needs of today's world. But intrinsic to the notion of human and political rights which England has supported longer than any other nation is that they are inalienable — not to be taken on and off like so many suits of clothes according to the needs of the season.

The role of communication in expression of political ideas and principles is crucial to understanding what is going on in England. We here in the US have a written constitution that guarantees us a basic Bill of Rights. In England, people have only the intangible whisper of custom, and custom can be swept easily away (written documents can be ignored too — but stubborn citizens can continue to point to them, as dissentniks did in the dark years in the Soviet Union.)

The gagging of the BBC shouts attention to a related aspect of this problem. The US has long been criticized for its commercial system of broadcasting. But the great strength of this commercialism is its independence from the government. The British system, always an adjunct of its government, can operate in a healthy way only as long as the government allows it to; in structure, this system has always been closer to the Soviet system of media control than to our system of little control. (The FCC, as indicated in chronicles such "Naughty Words and Obscene Censorship" and "Rock 'n' Roll vs. the Arbiters of Decency" unfortunately prevents my saying "no" control. Even so, the power of the FCC in America is a sliver of the British government's power over broadcasting in its country.) And now the robins of censorship are coming home to roost.

Democracy is always vulnerable to political leaders who see their mandate as making society safe — rather than open — from this or that. In the 1970s, Richard Nixon played such a role in our country. But the strength of our independent media — and independent Congress and Judiciary — beat this back.

Britain has now been deprived of the full operation of such media — thus giving us another powerful argument on behalf of decentralized media like personal computers and modems whose operation is less subject to governmental fiat.

CHIP-ON-MY-SHOULDER PARANOIA

Karl Popper — my favorite living philosopher — says that in order to best refute an argument, we should strive to present it as vividly and effectively as possible. In that spirit, I offer you the following scenario....

It begins with a simple and chilling insight: the revolution in interactivity and access can be turned against itself, and used as the ultimate vehicle in totalitarian domination. The key is that that which sends information from private homes and businesses to the external world can just as easily be used to monitor private homes and businesses... and indeed everything we do....

The first expression is a joint ruling of the Departments of Commerce and Transportation that all new personal computer chips must programmed to automatically send over modem and telephone copies of everything the users of these computers do.

Every electronic message sent, every comment entered in an online conference, every text composed offline on one's wordprocessor — these and everything else done with one's keyboard or mouse are automatically sent out to be stored in the government's new mega-giga-storage machine.

In the US, the four biggest personal computer manufacturers are IBM, Apple, Radio Shack, and Commodore. The last two go along with the ruling; the first two take the government to court. But a Supreme Court stacked by 12 years of Republican Presidents quickly supports the government on national security grounds. IBM reluctantly complies; Apple still refuses — but the government pressures bankers to freeze all Apple assets. Deprived of vital capital, unable to get either loans or investments, Apple folds within two years....

At the time of the ruling, some 100 million non-compliant machines already exist in the US. In a related ruling, the government insists that all new software must have a program that does the same thing as the new chips — i.e., automatically forwards all computer work to the central system. Within a year, 90 percent of the old machines are outfitted with the new software

--- their owners care more about being current with new software than about opening up their machines to government monitoring. This leaves some 10 million recalcitrants — many of whom have old CP/M machines. The government has a plan for these. The major bulletin boards and suppliers of public domain programs are knowingly and unknowingly infected with viruses which either put the recipient's machines out of business, or make them into government reporters like their more expensive cousins.

The online community and the academic community take a variety of stances. The big operations — like CompuServe and GEnie, like MIT and Columbia University — complain but ultimately comply with the government directive. The New School for Social Research and the New Jersey Institute of Technology do not.

FBI agents and government commando squads ring both places the next morning. At the New School in New York City, the Media Studies Program is able to stave off the attack for awhile — they cut the elevator cables, and gain a few hours of time on the 12th floor. Government agents finally make it up the stairs by the end of the day. Although most of the personnel have escaped down back doors and little known connectors between buildings, some of the administrative records of Media Studies and the Connect Ed Programs are now in government hands...

Meanwhile, out in Newark, Murray Turoff and the EIES staff make a valiant stand. But they are outnumbered and outgunned. A battery of explosives eventually breaks through, and the EIES "refrigerator" — the physical machine that houses the great EIES system — is blown up just as a new student is entering her first comment in the Connect Ed Cafe....

But this is the age of distributed systems — can't they foil the crackdown? No. One by the one they are hunted down. Since the long distance phone companies and data-packet services are all in the government's pocket, this proves to be relatively easy. Soon the distributed nodes are infected with viruses that either shut them down or spread the government's reporting program.

Foreign systems are the last hope. But most of these are quickly compromised by US government viruses. The new

Russian society, which has taken special pains to be as open to the computer revolution as possible, is especially vulnerable. In the United Kingdom, the Conservative government eagerly cooperates. Oxford and Cambridge and LSE computers are compromised. At the Open University, programmers manage to hide some valuable data in a faculty member masquerading as a dead body, but the OU system falls into government hands....

Now it's your turn: what's wrong with this?

DON'T DISTRACT ME
WITH THE FAX

Fax machines have been become office staples more quickly than any medium in history, including photocopiers and telephones. Part of this is due to our whetted appetites for any new technologies that we can personally control. Part of this is due to the ease with which a fax can be used.

Unlike the personal computer, whose effective operation requires some training, the fax can be used right out of the box — almost as easily as pressing a button. Since electronic mail (made possible via word processing and telecommunication capabilities of personal computers) and fax both deal with the transmission of text and graphics, and since the fax does this with much less effort, the fax has been hailed as a successor to electronic mail and even the personal computer. This is not so. Indeed, the fax will likely be an interesting and useful chapter in the story of text transmission — a story in which the personal computer and its adjuncts will continue to be central sections.

Fax or "facsimile" transmission from which fax gets its name is part of an ancient branch of media evolution which goes back to cave paintings and hieroglyphic writing and continues in modern times with the photograph and the LP. These media operate by literally copying as best as possible the object to be communicated: thus, the grooves on the LP literally resemble the highs and lows in the patterns of sounds they reproduce, and the pictograph and photograph look like the images they represent. This "lookability" — or "analogic" communication, to use the engineering term — gives these media instant recognition and enormous appeal. No one has to be taught how to read a photograph or a motion picture.

Beginning with the phonetic alphabet, however — indeed, with human spoken language — a radically different mode of communication arose, a mode which describes rather than copies the object to be communicated. Consider: the letters of the alphabet, and the sounds of our words, look nothing like the objects and ideas they describe. They are rather recipes for the reconstruction of these objects and ideas. The writer and reader must undergo some training in the use of these recipes; but once learned, the recipe method has far more power than the literal copying mode of communication. We master 26 letters and a limited number of rules for their recombination, and we write the words dog and god in a fraction of the time it would take to draw or produce pictures of these entities.

The "digital" processing of personal computers is part of this descriptive or recipe branch of media, as is the CD sound recording. In these media, a set of instructions for the recreation of the original, not a copy of the original, is what is being transmitted. Each time a digital medium is used, the original is recreated anew. This is why a CD recording never wears down: a recipe can be implemented an infinite number of times, with no wear and tear on the recipe. An "analogic" LP, in contrast, diminishes in quality slightly with each play.

The advantages of digital or personal computer processing of text are even more striking. The binary instructions which cause text to be produced or reproduced on screens and printers can be easily amended to produce revised versions that are as pristine as the original. These same binary instructions allow the words they produce to be searched for keywords and misspellings; permit dissemination of these words to an unlimited number of people at the same time; provide for storage of text electronically at a sliver of the space required for storage of paper. Most importantly, the binary recipe for one text can be linked to the binary codes of others, in fact to binary instructions for the recreation of graphics and sounds and other modes of human communication, thus creating the possibility of interlinked "hypertext" or "hypermedia" databases in which all elements of human knowledge are accessible and connected. Much like the human brain, which translates all the colors, sounds, and ideas that we come across into a same, interconnected internal language of its own understanding, so the digital processing of letters, images, and sounds gives them a common, interchangeable denominator.

Connected to digital personal computers (as in computer-fax boards), the fax is a part of this electronic text "natural" revolution. As a stand-alone copying device, the fax even when digital marches to an analogic drum, in that its task is the literal reproduction of the face of the document, rather than transmission of the underlying code — the words — from which the document is assembled. It has value to the degree that current computer technology cannot easily transmit codes for recreation of pictures and certain graphics, and in instances such as signatures, in which a screen reconstitution of the original could call into question its authenticity, and a literal paper copy is therefore preferable. Fax also is of great value in the transmission of a final document, for the purpose of closing and filing a discussion. But it is of far less value in transmission of a document in progress, where electronic text facilitates editing and recreation of the text as many times as necessary, by as many people with legitimate access as required, to get it right. Fax is, in a word, authoritarian, whereas electronic text is democratic. Much as I appreciate its convenience, I would therefore conclude that the future of fax as a stand-alone device, let alone a replacement for the personal computer, is limited.

At first glance, digital or recipe processing may seem to be less natural than the literal copying method. But a recipe technique is used by DNA every time it instructs proteins in its environment to assemble into a living organism. New lives are not copies of their parents, but fresh creations sprung from fresh recipes transmitted by their parents. We should not be surprised, then, to find digital processing a growing way of life in our technology.

A NEW YORK PHILOSOPHER
IN THE COURT OF THE AMISH

Tina and I and Simon and Molly just returned from a week in Lancaster County, Pennsylvania. We went there for little relaxation close at hand — the county is about two and a half hours from New York City by car — and a peek at the Amish and their way of life, which we thought would interest the kids. Our children were indeed enchanted by the horse and buggies that the Amish use as transportation, and their colorful dress. But what we found I also count as one of the most significant events of my scholarly life.

Most people, including philosophers of technology with whom I studied, consider the Amish an interesting oddity of throwbacks who have rejected all modern technology and have turned their back on the modern world. This popular stereotype is even more mistaken than these images usually are.

To begin with, the Amish are not one, but a variety of subtly and in some cases drastically different groups, with a wide range of attitudes towards modern devices. Most importantly, none have rejected technology outright — rather, they struggle with the appeal of technologies, usually accepting a new machine at first, agonizing over its real and projected social consequences, and then deciding whether and to what extent it can be used. In short, they come the closest to a living embodiment of philosophy of technology that I have ever seen (or read about).

In most cases, they in fact have decided to live with a new device, while straining the limits of human ingenuity to keep it from disrupting their social order. Electricity from central power companies is forbidden — sockets in the wall make the home and place of business an appendage of an uncontrollable, huge external political-economic power structure — but electricity from 12 volt self-sufficient batteries is all right. Phones are frowned upon (not absolutely forbidden) in the homes of most Amish, but since the 1930s, phone "shanties" on edges of property have been permitted. These are seen as affording most of the advantages of the phone, while strengthening communal use which they see as crucial to a healthy life. (In an observation which I thought only McLuhan, I, and a few other media theorists had made, the Amish see the public reach of the phone in private homes as an almost irresistible undoing of privacy; see my chronicle on "Flipped-Out Privacy and the Telephone.")

The modern age is of course no gentler to the Amish than it is to philosophers in the "English" world (the Amish name for all who do not share their high-German, circa 1690 Swiss roots). The Amish proscription on centrally supplied electricity dove-tailed nicely with their religious-ethical dislike of the content of mass media like television: when you unplug it and "put it away," you put away not only objectionable structure but offensive content. Now, however, a new device has crept into some Amish homes and businesses: an ingenious little "in-verter," which transforms 12 volt battery current into a reason-able likeness of the 110 volt power that comes from the socket. Bishop Beiler's 1919 ruling that anything that flows from a 12 volt battery is acceptable and anything that uses 110 volt power is not seems very precise. How exquisite and wrenching the paradox, then, when television and … yes, even computers … are connected by a few custom-abiding Amish into inversion 110 volt power. (Pocket calculators that run on batteries are already in very widespread use. As far as I could see, laptop pcs are not, and I found nothing about laptops in even the most recent literature about Amish life.)

As most of you know, my own philosophy of technology is very much at odds with that of the Amish. Confronted by the undeniable invasion of privacy of the phone, I say: invent an answering machine, or better yet, use fax and e-mail. In other words, rather than shattering the window to avoid its invitation to the Peeping Tom, invent and deploy a window shade.

But I find the Amish struggle with the modern world heroic and laudable nonetheless. While many people accept most technologies with open, unquestioning arms — coming to the right conclusion, from my perspective, via the wrong method — the Amish seem daily and keenly aware that humans have options with technologies, and these can be exercised. If the Amish and I differ radically in our underlying premises and actual assessments of technology (I believe it should be resisted only in the most extreme of cases — like nuclear weapons), we are in the same court regarding the importance of applying a critical judgement to what the human environment offers us.

And I do share something with the Amish in their distrust of central, prefabricated education, and their championship of education integrated with the home and business environment. This, after all, is what online education via personal computer and modem is all about.

PREAMBLE TO SOVIET CHRONICLES: AUGUST 1989

The times tremble with possibilities.

Mikhail Gorbachev has joined Jefferson and Kennedy as a leader whose actions and symbols have opened the world a bit wider for human expression. Not only is the Soviet Union changing — a change which by itself would be among the most important developments in our century — but the teleconnected nature of our century means that changes in the Soviet Union are inevitably changing the rest of the world. If the Soviet Union does not quite have free elections, Poland now just about does. China has taken a staggering step backwards, true, but the memory of all of us who watched the Chinese spring on television will not be persuaded in the least by the retelling of reality by Chinese authorities. Big Brother and *1984* meet their match in the cyberspace that we all share and, in the case of computer conferencing, contribute to in our own homes and places of business. For unlike Orwell's world, our interconnected realm is not completely controlled by central authorities. Indeed, our hallmark is a decentralization unknown at least since the time of Lascaux and Altamira.

The Soviet Union has already been a frequent subject of these Chronicles — for example, "SDI," "Amerika," and "Critical Media Coverage." Indeed, owing to the coincidence of Gorbachev coming to power just a few months before these Chronicles began, the Soviet Union depicted here has been a Soviet Union in sharp change. In the above three chronicles, Gorbachev moved from an outright adversary with great ideas to a leader outrightly worthy of our admiration, albeit still less than democratic.

At the same time, Connected Education has worked on a variety of unofficial projects with Soviet citizens. In the summer of 1988, I met in Boston with a Soviet ecologist and his student. Connect Ed people have been engaged in online discussion with Walt Roberts and his development of a "greenhouse glasnost" network — a series of computer conferences to discuss US-Soviet cooperation in reducing the possible greenhouse effect. And shortly after the earthquake in Armenia in December, I was invited by Soviet science advisor Yevgeny Velikov to take part in an online discussion on the Notepad system on how to best bring international relief to Armenia. (Velikov apparently heard about me in an article about Connected Education that appeared in the September 1988 *Smithsonian* magazine, and was translated and reprinted in the Soviet Union. Since participating in the Armenian online conferences, I have become good friends with Grigor Vaganian of the "SEARCH" center in Yerevan, and Grigor has been good enough to translate and publish several of my essays there.) We each contribute to the development of the new international mosaic in our own ways, and online communication and online education seem to have significant roles to play.

In the next months, perhaps years, I therefore hope to share with you a series of Chronicles that portray and reflect upon both the emergence of a new Soviet Union (and therefore new world) in general, and some of the specific experiences I've had, or will have, with this in particular. Owing to the very success of Connected Education in our graduate program at The New School for Social Research and other endeavors, I won't be able to enter chronicles here as frequently as I have in the past (certainly not on the often weekly or even biweekly basis). But I have a goodly number of snippets already on disk, and more in mind, so do keep posted.

The next Chronicle is my first vignette — an evening drive in Boston with a Soviet Ph.D. student that got me thinking about "Universality and Inanity"....

UNIVERSALITY AND INANITY

Picture this. You're in a strange neighborhood in a big city. It's about 10:30 in the evening, you're driving around lost in a car that's just about out of gas, and your passenger is a Soviet doctoral candidate whom you met for the first time a few hours earlier. You speak no Russian, and he speaks a bit of English. You're supposed to deliver your passenger to his friend's house somewhere on some street that neither of you can seem to locate. You've been driving around in circles for an hour. Finally, you decide to flag down a cop.

"Well, at least we won't be arrested," I make a lame attempt at humor. Mikhail doesn't laugh. I can't tell if he didn't like the joke, or didn't understand the language. At this point, I'm not even sure what the joke was myself — I don't really think that people get arrested in the Soviet Union just for asking the police instructions, do I...?

The officer approaches. Meanwhile, a group of panhandlers, seeing our parked car but not the officer, approach from the other side.

Now Mikhail chuckles. "We have Asians in the Soviet Union too," he says, as the street people notice the officer and leave.

I explain where we want to go, and listen intently as the officer gives us detailed instructions. I have a good general sense of direction, but I'm terrible at taking down these sorts of instructions. I look at Mikhail after the officer leaves. No point asking him if he got what the officer was saying.

I start driving. "No, no," Mikhail says, "you want to turn that way."

"You sure?"

"Yes."

Like I said, I'm terrible at these sorts of instructions, so I'm willing to take a chance even with Mikhail. We apparently got off on the wrong exit leading from Logan Airport to the Mass

Turnpike, and have a ways to go. The needle's flirting with empty, and not a single gas station that we pass is open.

"So you're a doctoral candidate," I figure I might as well put the time to good use. "What exactly does that mean?"

In the US, a doctoral candidate is someone who has finished all of his or her coursework for the Ph.D., and has "just" the dissertation or thesis (a book-length research paper) needed for completion of the degree. Some souls stay stuck forever in this academic form of purgatory.

"You have a Ph.D., right?" Mikhail says to me. I shake my head yes. "Well," he continues, "I already have something similar, though not quite as rigorous as your degree." He describes to me an educational system that I had already vaguely heard about. Their Ph.D. is somewhere between our Masters and Ph.D., and is attained by a fair number of scholars and scientists. The holders of this degree are called "doctor," as are holders of Ph.D.'s here. But the Soviet Union also offers a degree even more advanced than the Ph.D. — one which takes years of study and work even to qualify for, and which is awarded to only a small number of advanced scholars. This is the degree that Mikhail is a candidate for. I'm impressed, especially since Mikhail looks to be not much more than in his early 30s.

We begin talking about the dissertation process. To me, the most absurd part of this process was the final oral defense: a group of professors, none of whom have read your dissertation in its entirety, few of whom have read it at all, grill you for several hours on issues that they think should have been covered in your dissertation. The successful candidate must grit his or her teeth, and play along with this — for to do otherwise, to risk an outburst of raw truth, would be to jeopardize years of work.

Now Mikhail and I are both laughing, together. "You mean they don't read the dissertations here, either? I thought this was another unique quality of the Soviet bureaucracy." (His English wasn't that polished, but this conveys the thrust of what he said.)

Somehow, Mikhail and I had discovered a common ground far more vivid and real than the many discussions I had had with Soviets earlier. Two systems, as different from one another (prior to Gorbachev) as political, economic, and social systems can be, had nonetheless an identical oppressive inanity in the academic process. Our lingua franca was the academic theatre of the absurd, a farce that creative scholars must submit to whatever the language of the directors. The positivists and Kantians and Popperians were right after all: the pursuit of knowledge is indeed ultimately universal and transcendent of cultural conditioning.

Discovery of this root was immensely liberating for both of us, certainly for me. It reminds me, in retrospect, of the first time I realized, talking to a woman, that men and women shared a whole bunch of very similar feelings.

We soon arrived at Mikhail's friend's house (under his expert guidance). We promised to stay in touch.

I found an open gas station right around the corner from his friend's house, and drove back to Cape Cod with the windows open in the early hours of that heady, warm summer morning...

[Note: "Mikhail" was not the real name of my passenger — I've changed it lest the discussion about doctoral readers cause him any embarrassment back home. Everything else in the above account is as it was.]

THREE CITIES AND T. REX

The disasters in Chernobyl, Yerevan (and throughout Armenia), and San Francisco provide important clues about the appropriate human relationship to technology.

The events in the first — Chernobyl — seem to offer a clearcut warning about the dangers of high technology. And they do. But we should also take note that that the deaths resulting from Chernobyl were at most 1/25th of those resulting from the earthquake in Armenia. Similarly, the deaths in San Francisco were a fraction of those in Armenia. Even a single unnecessary human death is tragic and unacceptable; but there is profound meaning, I think, in the differences in the above numbers.

The difference between San Francisco and Armenia can be summed up as high tech vs. low tech: San Francisco's casualties were far less than Armenia's because the tall, high-tech structures of San Francisco were designed to sway without crumbling. A "no-tech" environment of no structures at all would likely be more earthquake resistant in some ways, but this is not a serious option (in that people are generally unable to live without some shelter). Thus, the role of human control of technology becomes clear: move forward and ahead, transform from low tech to high tech. The notion of freezing technology, or de-technologizing society in some way, is literally fatal when the technology is frozen in the low-tech state of Armenia at the time of its quake. In contrast to the quake-wise buildings in San Francisco, the constructions in Armenia collapsed like a deadly deck of cards.

Yet high-tech environments continue to frighten us. Is this fear justified? Three Mile Island resulted in few if any significant casualties, and Chernobyl resulted in far less death than in Armenia. Fission energy — though in need of replacement by safer fusion and solar sources — has been far less deadly to date than natural disasters like earthquakes and plagues. (See "A Fire Not Worth It" in these Chronicles for more on my opposition to fission energy.) And has the Valdez oil spill, for all its damage to the environment, resulted in any human casualties? No immediate human casualties, and probably far fewer animal casualties than human casualties in Armenia. (Bhopal resulted in high casualties — but here the technology was also "low-tech," in this case, chemical.)

What do I conclude on the basis of this?: (1) that the greatest dangers to human beings continue to be natural not human in origin; (2) that less advanced technologies can greatly aggravate natural dangers (another example would be urban conditions in medieval Europe that stoked the Black Plague); (3) that more advanced technologies, while certainly in need of continuous scrutiny, are the best hope for human improvement.

Meanwhile the discovery of the most complete Tyrannosaurus rex skeleton to date, reported in today's *NY Times*, speaks to us about these same points. Just this Sunday my family and I admired the Tyrannosaurus skeleton — found in the same Montana area — that stands in the American Museum of Natural History in New York City. These mute, magnificent creatures, whose bones amaze and thrill our eyes, are telling us something.

What are they saying to us through their bones through the ages?

That nature without technology-producing-brains is not enough.

No one knows what ended the reign on Earth of these creatures, but whatever natural disaster it was, the dinosaurs were unable to do much about it. They, like every other living thing on Earth save humans, are obliged to repeat their behaviors over and over again. If the environment changes slowly enough, then perhaps the blind suggestions of genetic mutation will provide a remedy — a suitable new behavior. But when the environment changes quickly — when the Earth literally moves beneath their feet — all organisms on Earth save us are obliged to fall into the crack.

We, on the other hand, build San Francisco's, and rebuild Armenia's, and someday if we keep working at it may build spaceships that take us far off this Earth altogether. And therein lies our hope.

THERAPY FOR THE HAND
THAT SHOOTS ITSELF IN THE FOOT

Catching up on my reading of some old *Science* magazines the other day, I came across one of those stories which, while really not in the least bit funny, had to make me laugh.

From what we now know were the closing days of the Cold War, the October 4, 1985 issue reported that then Defense Secretary Caspar Weinberger was "absolutely delighted" with the successful test of a preliminary Star Wars type anti-satellite device.* Seems the Air Force was able to use this device to reduce an old solar monitoring satellite to rubble. The satellite had been deemed "marginally operable" by Air Force evaluators beforehand, which apparently was why it was chosen as a suitable target for the test.

This came as a surprise, however, to solar research scientists under the impression that they were very much actively working with the slain satellite. David Bohlin, head of NASA's solar physics section, said he had mixed feelings about the 'successful' test — happiness as a patriotic American, sadness as a scientist to see an old, still operational servant so rudely destroyed. Another solar physicist pointed out that although the satellite wasn't glamorous, it was still dutifully pumping back data at the time it met its creator(s). My first feelings when I read this story were that I hoped our online science colleagues in Boulder and Tucson didn't have any important research blown up with this flying workhorse.

Human error, like noise and breakdown in the universe, is of course ubiquitous, and can never be completely eliminated. But the likelihood of errors of this sort can certainly be reduced by better communication among all concerned parties. And the pity is that we already have the means for this improved communication at hand.

Clearly with a test of this sensitivity, the Air Force can not be expected to make a general public announcement of its plans. Nor can the scientists, who apparently were not consulted before the test, be expected to notify the Defense Department that such and such a satellite is still very much in usage, just in case Defense has plans to blow it up.

But how about placing the progress and results of all research involving difficult-to-keep-track-of laboratories like satellites in online databases? These reports could be carefully encrypted to keep away prying eyes before formal publication, but their existence would oblige the Air Force or any other agency seeking to take out a satellite to check the record before shooting. Perhaps Defense would have decided to use the solar satellite as a target anyway, but at least their decision would have been informed, and without the tragicomic elements of this episode.

It has long been a cliché that our technological powers often outstrip our ability to control them. Nor is this bad — the cycle of creating a technology first, and then straining to catch up to and understand its capabilities may be a very healthy evolutionary strategy in a universe in which deliberate design so often fails. Indeed, to the extent that we already understand and control an environment, a new technology is a limited value — technologies are most needed precisely in those areas where we currently have little control (as in destruction of incoming missiles — still a possibility in this yet dangerous world).

But neither can we afford to be a dumb, bumbling giant, with little or no control of our huge technological muscles. We've got to start paying attention to building up a societal and Earth-wide level nervous system through which we can convey information and therein better control these muscles.

Way back in the 1840s, Nathaniel Hawthorne wrote about the telegraph turning the Earth into one big brain. We've had the technological wherewithal to communicate more effectively for quite some time, but as yet we've implemented only a small part of it. Time we got cracking.

Whatever the political shape of our world in the next decades, some sort of defense for the errant or maliciously launched missile will still be a necessity; whatever the scientific shape of our world, one hopes that the space in our solar system will be teeming with humans and satellites and stations. The next victim of a well-intended but poorly researched defense test could be a lot more costly than a workhorse solar-monitor satellite.

In the meantime, let's hope that none of the geo-stationary telecommunications satellites upon which much of our communications depend have been targeted.

---

*January, 1992: I favored and still favor development of an SDI system — now as a defense against a terrorist or bandit-nation missile. See my "SDI" chronicle in this volume for more on my views of space-based defense.

TELEWAR

Television coverage is not the least of the new technologies playing an important role in the Gulf War.

Television itself is of course not new. Neither is the immediate, continuous coverage we have come to associate with election nights and assassinations. But even assassinations have clearly defined endings, however shocking their beginnings may be.

A war in progress, however much we and its planners may want to project a definite timeline and ending, is by definition a highly uncertain, open-ended event. We have an insatiable need to know what is going on — and television coverage to some extent exacerbates this need, for it on the one hand provides us with lots of information, but in a form that leaves us feeling nonetheless uninformed. We thus are to our ocean of information on TV much the same as the Ancient Mariner is to his ocean of "water, water, everywhere, nor any drop to drink..."

The primary problem of television coverage of real events is that it is a one-way coverage, that pumps us with images and information, but gives us no way of questioning this information. We thus are obliged to rely on the talent of television commentators, who at their best may indeed ask of their interviewees questions that we may have in mind, but can never touch all the questions that any given person may want to ask. Deprived of this ability to refine our understanding via active dialogue, television viewers are thus left to fend for themselves in coming to terms with a barrage of reports that can mean life and death to their loved ones.

Another problem with television coverage is that even sophisticated viewers tend to accept what they see on TV as true. We may know, as a matter of logic, that a report is unconfirmed or speculative. But because seeing is indeed a large part of believing, we accept that report as true on an emotional level. Viewers of NBC-TV on the evening of January 17 lived through a nerve-gas SCUD attack on Israel — a harrowing experience only partially diminished by the later news that the reports of nerve gas had been incorrect. Far more important than the specific words, and far more searing to the soul, were images of mothers putting gas masks on their children, and reporters putting on gas masks in the midst of their reporting.

The frustrating part of the problem with television coverage is that there is probably not much that we can or should do about it. No information at all may be preferable to misleading information, but the information on television is by no means entirely misleading. Our best course of action probably lies in giving the television viewer better skills with which to deal with this presentation of information — an education of the viewer that is the responsibility of everyone, most especially television.

THE COMMUNITY OF FREEDOM:
AUGUST 1991

And freedom, oh freedom,
well that's just some people talking.
Your prison is walking
through this world all alone....

— "Desperado," Randy Newman

The above articulates the best spirit of communism — that freedom, classically defined, is not enough; that without a community to be part of, we're all prisoners of isolation. The economic counterpart of this psychological truth was expressed well at the beginning of this century by Anatole France, who asked what good is freedom, if it's freedom to starve?

But communism failed, because its practitioners failed to recognize two other truths: one, that while freedom may not be enough, it is nonetheless still essential; and two, that freedom unprotected is vulnerable to personal greed for power that ends up crushing the benefits of community at first gained.

Most people outside of the Soviet orb found this out in the actions of Stalin in the late 1930s and after. Close relatives of my parents' generation, who as progressive young humanitarians had supported American and international communism in the 1930s, were horrified at Stalin's pact with Hitler, and the utter lack of principle this bespoke. In retrospect, this was but the tip of an iceberg of cold mass murder and utter destruction of community.

Thomas Jefferson, of course, understood this fully, and attempted to implement this understanding in a Bill of Rights which made freedom of expression inviolable. But Jefferson was old hat in the 20th century even in America, where Oliver Wendell Holmes ruled that speech that provoked a clear and present danger to life or property could be abridged notwithstanding the First Amendment. Hugo Black insisted to his death that Holmes was wrong — that "Congress shall make no law" limiting freedom of speech meant just that, no law — but his was an isolated voice.

Still, the reservoir of Jeffersonian respect for freedom of press in this country was enough, in the end, to stop Richard Nixon's all-out assault on the press in the Pentagon Papers case. His partner in detente, Leonid Brezhnev, had no such tradition of restraint — indeed, quite the contrary with Stalin — and when the end came to that system, it was quite total and fully deserved. The August 1991 right wing coup against Gorbachev gambled that the new found love of freedom in that country was less than the love of food on the shelves, and the coup lost.

And what of the communist ideal of community? Can it be pursued and attained without sacrifice of freedom? The new Soviet Union, or whatever that area of the world will be called, shows that the sense of community is strong there, indeed far stronger than ever before. It is a community of self-interest able to stand up to tanks and totalitarians. It is a community beset by so many problems that in many ways it is barely a community. But it is undeniably a community in what is likely the most profound sense of all: it is a community of freedom.

VIDEO TEMPOS

The peculiar role of electronic media — elected by no one, yet accorded in retrospect a central position in our democracy by Jefferson and the founding fathers — has long been suspect in international affairs and crises. As early as 1934, Lewis Mumford in *Technics and Civilization* saw instantaneous electronic communication of events opening floodgates of kneejerk reactions that would reduce our civilization to bestiality. The delay of print and physical transport of paper was crucial, Mumford argued — a saving buffer in human affairs that afforded the time and space necessary for contemplation and reason.

Not that the world had done so well under the print regime. The Battle of New Orleans was fought after the peace treaty ending the War of 1812 had been signed in Paris, and the slow, slow fuse leading to the First World War did nothing to reduce its eventual severity.

Still, the feeling lingers that instantaneous global coverage can feed as much as starve a problem — as in satisfaction of the publicity motives in terrorism, and portrayal of a biological weapons factory as a baby food plant in Iraq in the Gulf War. And closer to home, in a related line of criticism, television continues to take hits for placing so much value on cosmetic leadership.

Although such objections to the media have merit, I think they miss the bigger picture. For the feature most valuable in an electronic environment is not appearance at all, but the ability to respond quickly and decisively — as rapidly as the initial events themselves take place and are conveyed by the media. The agonizing example of Jimmy Carter during the Iranian hostage crisis shows how heavy is the political toll for delay in an electronically connected world. The swing in George Bush's popularity from its heights during his decisive action in the Gulf War to the depths owing to his indecision regarding the economy in 1991 is a more recent example.

Sometimes the myth of appearance — the political illusion that media make appearance all important — masks the real reasons for success in media and politics. JFK did indeed look and sound good on television. But he also unearthed an April of new endeavors — ranging from the Peace Corps to space — and the accurate reporting of these, not that JFK looked good, was and is the main reason for his popularity then and now. Similarly, Ronald Reagan may indeed have been the "great communicator," but his action in first stoutly opposing the Soviets, and then being quick to embrace the Gorbachev initiative, was the key factor, in my view, in his becoming the most popular president since JFK. (See "Critical Media Coverage vs. Great Impulse Leadership" for further discussion of these issues.)

The upshot is this: Our fast-paced media environment makes mistakes, can exacerbate problems with its coverage, but most of all it seems to select for survival those leaders who can keep pace and play more than a passive role in events the media report.

Is this bad? Should we worry about reflex-reaction leaders who may put the world at jeopardy?

I don't think so. The point is that events are likely to continue occurring fast and furiously regardless of what the media do. News coverage may have played a role in igniting the fire, but it's already lit and moving. What we need most are leaders who can think and act quickly and forcefully enough to see that the fire burns for humanity's good. Whether Mumford would like it or not, the 21st century will not be a time for leisurely contemplation.

CLASSIFIED:
PHILOSOPHY OF TECHNOLOGY

The world has come a long way in the most profound ways in the past few years. I suppose most scholars and educators in the international arena have personal benchmarks that give measure to this progress — some event or incident, small or large, that indicates to us on an individual level how connected the human family has become since the disintegration of the totalitarian Soviet Union.

For me, a letter I received in the Fall of 1985 from Novosibirsk in the Soviet Union, from someone I didn't know, provides such a benchmark. The letter requested in usual scholarly fashion a copy of my paper, "Information Technologies as Vehicles of Evolution."

Coincidentally, almost to the same day, I found a public announcement on EIES — the Electronic Information Exchange System (online system that was the first home of Connected Education) — cautioning all users that a few Soviets were now on the system, and we would be held responsible, under US Commerce Department regulations, for any trade secrets we might advertently or inadvertently divulge. "Information Technologies" existed not only as an article in the journal *Technology in Society* (my Soviet correspondent had likely seen an index of the journal's contents), but right there online, and the request for my paper could have come from one of the online Soviets rather than a distant, unknown person in a Soviet city I'd barely heard of.

What would I have done, given such an online request? I like to think my work contains some important insights into the technological process, though to be sure nothing concrete enough to be classified as a trade secret. Still, the warning — and the statute — about discussion with the Russians would have given me some pause, and certainly added at least a drop of anxiety to what otherwise would have been a happy event in a scholar's life.

I remember thinking at the time that maybe I ought to grow up, and recognize the sort of real world we live in. Who cares about my egotism as a scholar, or even my altruism in wanting to spread the benefits of knowledge, when compared to the lack of freedom in the Soviet regime, their antagonistic world posture, and the damage an American could conceivably do in this regard by giving this regime some valuable information about, say, computer conferencing.

Here was my answer: although information technologies, like most devices, have their weapon applications, their use throughout history has generally been a liberating one. Especially in the case of personal media, their introduction into societies has generally been a thorn in the side of the repressive totalitarian approach. The Xerox machine, to use one example, caused Soviet leaders more problems than 50 years of underground radio and bootleg presses. So let the Soviets have some of our telecommunication technology: if dissentnik groups got a bulletin board going, it might have an even greater effect there than the widely circulated Xerox handouts. (See my "Samizdat Video" in these Chronicles for more on the effect of information technologies on totalitarian regimes.)

We lived in a strange world, then. The heads of countries met in summits, but the citizens were supposed to stay cowering behind their national boundaries, more ludicrous than the overwhelmed Dutch boy trying to stem the flow of information with his finger in the dike. Let's de-summitize the summit process, I argued: let individuals in ideologically opposing societies have their own summits, whether through computer conferencing, or exchange of papers, or personal visits. Brave but empty words for a scholar on an online system: words that had no chance of reaching the people in power.

Like I said, maybe I should have grown up and faced the real world.

Fortunately, the world grew up for me.

And now we have Helena Gourko, Professor of Philosophy, online with us from Minsk, Byelorussia, teaching a course for Connected Education. Interaction among all kinds of people, scholars and otherwise, is common. But we shouldn't forget the dissemination of scholarly information in even the worst days of the Cold War, information that helped in some way to make this possible.

Oh yes, I sent a copy of my paper to Novosibirsk back in 1985.

Never heard anything more. But someday I hope to meet my colleague in philosophy across the world and pass some secrets about Kant's *Critique of Pure Reason*.

SAMIZDAT VIDEO REVISITED

Most of us think of Madonna and Michael Jackson when we think of videos. Significant as their role in popular culture might be, the role of videos back in the heyday of the Soviet Union in the early 1980s may have been of greater significance politically.

The waning of old totalitarian-encouraging technologies of one-way mass broadcasting, and the rise of consumer controlled modules that foster decentralization and opposition to top-down societies, has actually been going on for well more than a decade. The Soviet Union was once able to stifle criticism of its Afghanistan policy in the ranks of Radio Moscow by simply insisting that no commentator ever be left alone in a broadcast booth. Cassettes are more resistant to government domination, for once distributed they are quite beyond the power of any government to disfigure or jam. And once hooked up to a TV monitor, they carry all the persuasive presence and stimulation of a broadcast program. So even before Gorbachev's revolution, samizdat videos were telling a story to the Soviet people in sharp opposition to government sponsored versions of reality.

Of course, to make use of videocassettes, one must have equipment capable of at least playing and preferably reproducing the videos. And such equipment is a good deal more sophisticated than the simple passive one-way receivers that serve as TV sets for most of the world. So we clearly had a difficult situation regarding the Soviet Union (one of many), where we would have been obliged to swallow the pill of sharing an advanced technology in order to give their people a better vehicle with which to express their impulses for freedom. Officially, at least, we opted to say no to this pill.

A common myth, by the way — arising mainly from Orwell's now quite expired *1984* — is that oppressive societies use advanced communications media to shore up their power. To the contrary, the low communications quotient of Germany made it especially vulnerable to Goebbels' manipulations in the '30s. Burning of books and bathing in one-way radio broadcasts fostered an environment in which the herd instinct rode at its highest. Hitler, as McLuhan pointed out, would not have been possible without uni-dimensional radio broadcasting his impassioned talks like a father to his children; fortunately, the same tribal beat of radio also brought unprecedented power to FDR and Winston Churchill. Meanwhile, the technological sophistication of the Allies allowed us to break the German Enigma code and win the war. (The Enigma code was cracked by Alan Turing who, not coincidentally, was also responsible for helping with the foundations of what eventually would become the personal computer, the biggest decentralizing agent of our century. The British society's thanks to him for this double-service was to hound him as a homosexual in the 1950s, but that's another story.)

Content, McLuhan also tells us in *Understanding Media*, is juicy meat thrown before us by technology that diverts us from its real effect — the revolutionizing consequences of its structure on our lives. The naive propagandist thinks to instigate people to action by merely telling or showing them things — content — that should rile them up against their leaders. This was the Radio Free Europe approach, whose years of earnest broadcasting likely had more effect on the broadcasters than the recipients.

A more sophisticated approach is to place in people's lives devices — not content — whose operation can make a difference. Devices through which people can express and disseminate their own solutions to their peculiar problems, rather than passively receive lessons in democracy from the outside (such passive reception itself being a lesson in anti-democracy).

No one likes to see an ideological opponent benefit from a technology that you have sweated to develop. Still, we must recognize that the most effective way of democratizing the world, and keeping it so, is to make available to the world whatever tools we can offer in support of democratic process — for tools, as John Dewey recognized, are often more central than ideas in human affairs.

The people in the once Soviet Union are finding their way to democracy; we'll likely never know what role samizdat video and like decentralizing media played in the early stages of this process. But totalitarian regimes still exist in other parts of the world — the human species is still far richer in the idea of democracy than the tools of its practice.

I thus hope Sony and IBM and their smaller cousins do all in their power to saturate the world with their wondrous amplifiers of the individual mind and will.

THE END OF SOVIET TECHNOLOGY?

The dissolution of the Soviet Union, whatever new confederation it gives rise to, inevitably entails the disruption of one of the great technological powers of the 20th century. As new leaders struggle to set up democratic and capitalist structures — which can lead to technological progress in the long run — much of the recent fruit of Marxist technology will turn sour and rot. This applies not only to nuclear missiles any sane person is glad to be rid of, but to cosmonauts on the cutting edge of the human movement into space, who in many ways have already been left stranded.

Technological decline in the Soviet Union actually predates its breakup by several years, and may indeed be in part responsible for the death of Communism there. Harrison Salisbury wrote in the *New York Times Magazine* that Soviet leaders in the aftermath of Chernobyl began to lose confidence in the human ability to constructively guide and control technology. The blame for Chernobyl was in many Soviet quarters apparently placed not on nuclear fission technology in particular, but on the technological enterprise in general. Modern technology may be barrelling beyond our power, one Soviet official told Salisbury several years ago, citing Three Mile Island and the Challenger as incidence of the same problem in the United States.

Reasons to be pleased by the despair of Soviet technology are not hard to come by. Beyond the narrowly patriotic view of the technological high ground now left to the West, philosophic critics of technology have long been urging the world to recognize the inherently autonomous, out-of-control nature of technology. Writers like Jacques Ellul (*The Technological Society*) and Langdon Winner (*Autonomous Technology*) presumably would welcome the decomposition of one of these "out-of-control" systems.

Not I. Although I disagreed — and disagree — to the point of contempt with virtually the entire economic/political program of Marxism, I've always admired the aspect of Marxist philosophy which holds that, through technological manipulation of the environment, humans may continually improve their economic and spiritual wellbeing (i.e., their physical comfort and their understanding of life). Marx, whatever his self-impressions, was inextricably a product of the high Victorian age of progress in science and invention — an age that brought us telegraphs, telephones, phonographs, photographs, motion pictures, and ultimately automobiles, radios, air travel, and the Darwinian, Freudian, and Einsteinian revolutions. The concept of progress has had a rocky course in the West since then, but the Soviet Union — despite its totalitarian climate — was faithful to this Victorian ideal.

In fact, the totalitarian perception — as distinct from the philosophic/humanistic thread of Marx on technology — is quite compatible with Ellulian *attacks* on technology, or the view that Technology with a capital T is beyond human control, for in the eyes of the totalitarian, most differences and subtleties in human life become levelled into one. In reality, of course, there is no such thing as "Technology" (or "La Technique," as Ellul puts it): we have rather a myriad of devices — telephones, automobiles, air planes —most of which are firmly within our control, some of which are a bit harder to guide, and a very few of which are on the verge of going beyond us. Once upon a time we invented a marvelous device called the window. It allowed us both the shelter of the wall and the visibility of open space. But it also brought into being the Peeping Tom — and compromised our privacy. So we invented the window shade — just as centuries later we invented the telephone answering machine to screen the public's informational access to our homes. Windows and phones, then, are typical technologies — firmly within our power, and our ability to ameliorate or alter if troublesome.

Nuclear fission, alas, is not. Or rather, the consequences when something goes wrong are too great to justify the risk. Peeping Toms and obscene callers are nuisances; thousands contaminated with radiation in an area perhaps despoiled for centuries is an unacceptable obscenity.

The Soviet Union was thus right to be haunted by Chernobyl — we in the West would be wise to be a bit more haunted by it too. That Soviet Union — the one that not only engendered Chernobyl, but at first failed to report it and refused help from the West for critical hours — that Soviet Union deserved its fate, for that was the Soviet Union of totalitarian technology.

But not so the Soviet Union that launched the first satellites and Yuri Gagarin and led the first human encounter with space. That Soviet Union was, in its achievement, among humanity's finest hours in this or any century.

So I mourn the loss of the country, thinking, impulse, whatever it was, that brought us Sputnik.

When it comes to space, we've pretty much got the field to ourselves now. I'm not sure that's cause for celebrating. I hope we're up to it.

"JFK" AND GORBACHEV:
JANUARY, 1992

We come now to the last chronicle in this volume — also the first chronicle written with the knowledge that there would *be* a volume of these chronicles, thanks to Anamnesis Press.

Though the explicit theme of most of these chronicles has been technology — especially new information technologies — the real subject has been people, because technologies are after all only worthy of our notice and study to the extent that they make a difference in our lives.

Two people are especially in my mind this morning after New Year's.

JFK, the movie by Oliver Stone, not so much the person, is the subject of much controversy. I'm the first to admit the enormously distorting power of docudrama — indeed, I teach this regularly in both my "Media and Propaganda" and "Popular Culture and the Media" courses in person at the New School and online. Years before *JFK*, I noted how Robert Duvall's portrayal of Ike in the TV docudrama of the same name made Dwight Eisenhower seem much more dynamic and thoughtful than I remembered him to be. No doubt that Kevin Costner's portrayal of former New Orleans DA Jim Garrison does similar things to Garrison — not to mention the invention of scenes and speeches whole cloth in the name of dramatic license.

Critics are howling that Stone is distorting our recollection of the JFK assassination. *Newsweek* calls *JFK* twisted truth in its cover story, and the day before last I received a call from a columnist for *US News and World Report*, seeking my counsel in an article that would brand *JFK* as propaganda.

Of course it is — as is all documentary, and even news coverage, which after all shows us the world not "the way it was," but the way the editors put the pieces of "was" together for us to see. I suppose news reporting and journalism make more of an attempt to bring us the truth than do docudramas, and thus they have some legitimacy in critiquing docudramas like *JFK*,

202 · Paul Levinson

yet: What have the news media done to bring us the story of the assassination of John F. Kennedy? Little more than a passive conveyance of the highlights of the Warren Commission Report. Where is the muckraking journalism to get at records under government seal until well into the next century? Where is the outrage at a story that one demented loser could blow away a president single-handedly? Where is the thirst to either show this incredible story to be true (unlikely, in my view), or get at the real factors behind the Kennedy assassination, whatever they may be?

This energy, as far as I can see, is now being directed at Oliver Stone — who made a movie about a tragedy in our century that we have yet to recover from. Our space program is crippled, our political process compromised, and the media's response by and large is to pounce upon the one public person who has had the vision to make us think about this. I say: hats off to Stone, whatever the distortion of his movie. And to the media: go after the real story in this. Get us a look at those sealed documents so we can have a better idea of what happened to JFK.

Meanwhile, on the other side of the world, history is made because a Soviet leader left office unassassinated — or at least alive and in possession of his dignity.

I have written a lot about Mikhail Gorbachev in these chronicles — but so important has he been to our species that there is a lot more that I didn't have the chance to say.

Like in December, 1989, when the Berlin Wall came down and Eastern Europe threw off the dying hand of totalitarian rule. We bought a tape for our kids that December — "Wee Sing in Sillyville" — filled with happy children's songs about singing and living together, and respecting everyone's differences. I remember switching from the tape to the news coverage of Europe, and thinking that somehow, against all odds and predictions, these fairytales were now coming true. This was due to Gorbachev. There were tears in my eyes.

There were tears in my eyes of a different kind when I looked at my newborn son in 1983, and wondered why this new life that

I held in my hands had to be hostage to sick nuclear missiles aimed at us from across the world. I myself was born into pretty much the same sick world in 1947 — a world which I had no hand in making — and I felt ashamed on my son's behalf for our species.

But Gorbachev changed that. Others were responsible too — Reagan certainly deserves much credit — but none as much as Gorbachev. What exquisite irony, what drama worthy of Shakespeare, that this absolute dictator started the ball rolling in the military standdown — ordered this in fact — and ordered too the move towards democratization that eventually was his undoing.

Gorbachev made a lot of mistakes. But he took our world back a big step from suicide, and took away that bit of self-shame and self-anger that I used to have in my heart sometimes when I looked at my children.

And for that he will always have my gratitude.

ABOUT THE AUTHOR

Paul Levinson, Ph.D., is President of Connected Education, Inc., an international organization headquartered near New York City that offers courses for academic credit entirely via personal computer and modem in cooperation with The New School for Social Research, Polytechnic University of New York, and other institutions. He is on the Senior Faculty in the Graduate Media Studies Program at the New School for Social Research. He is author of *Mind at Large: Knowing in the Technological Age* (JAI Press, 1988), editor of *In Pursuit of Truth: Essays on the Philosophy of Karl Popper* (Humanities Press, 1982), and has published more than 50 articles on the philosophy and history of technology, and several science fiction short stories. He is Editor-in-Chief of the *Journal of Social and Biological Structures.* He lives with his wife and two children near New York City; they spend summers in a cottage by the bay on Cape Cod.

INDEX

"McCloud, Sam," 36
McLuhan, Marshall, 19, 39, 68, 106, 124, 125, 156, 174, 196
McNeill, William, 70
medical technology, 27-28, 117-118, 143-147
Mercer, Gail, 158
Meyrowitz, Joshua, 48, 57, 137
Miami Vice, 36, 40, 113-114, 129
Midler, Bette, 83
Miller, Dennis, 128
Mind at Large, 85, 91, 121
Minitel, 163
Mitcham, Carl, 87
Montessori, Maria, 46
Morgenthau, Robert, 161
Morrison, Jim, 36
movies (cinema, film, motion pictures), 30, 50, 67, 90, 104, 105, 113, 119-120, 126-127, 128, 133-134, 135, 154, 164
"multi-mediation," 80
multi-tasking, 133-134
Mumford, Lewis, 190, 191
Murphy's Law, Levinson's Addendum to, 34
Murrow, Edward R., 50-52
music, 37, 38, 57, 60, 66-67, 79, 82-84, 89-90, 113-114, 135, 154-156; *see also* Beatles; rock 'n' roll
myth, 126, 190, 195

NASA, 63-65, 87-88, 183; *see also* Challenger; space
nature, 23, 118; *see also* Cape Cod; evolution; extinction; technological risk
Nazi Germany, 116, 122, 136, 196
NBC-TV, 59-60, 113, 128, 186
New Jersey Institute of Technology, 32, 42, 158, 168
New Outlook, The, 154
New School for Social Research, The, 23, 31, 158, 168, 177, 201
New Year's, 40, 201